MAKING TOYS FOR SCHOOL-AGE CHILDREN

Using Ordinary Stuff for Extraordinary Play

Linda G. Miller
Mary Jo Gibbs

Illustrated by Kathy Dobbs

Dedication

From Mary Jo Gibbs

My personal thanks

To my friends--Rose, Angela, Janie, Sharon, Emily, Claire, Tami, Maria, Teri, and Jeanne--thanks for your support and encouragement! You are so special to me.

From Linda Miller

For creative teachers everywhere, and to those who (like me) like to see some directions. Happy teaching!

From Kathy Dobbs

For my husband Dale and son Sam—I love you both!

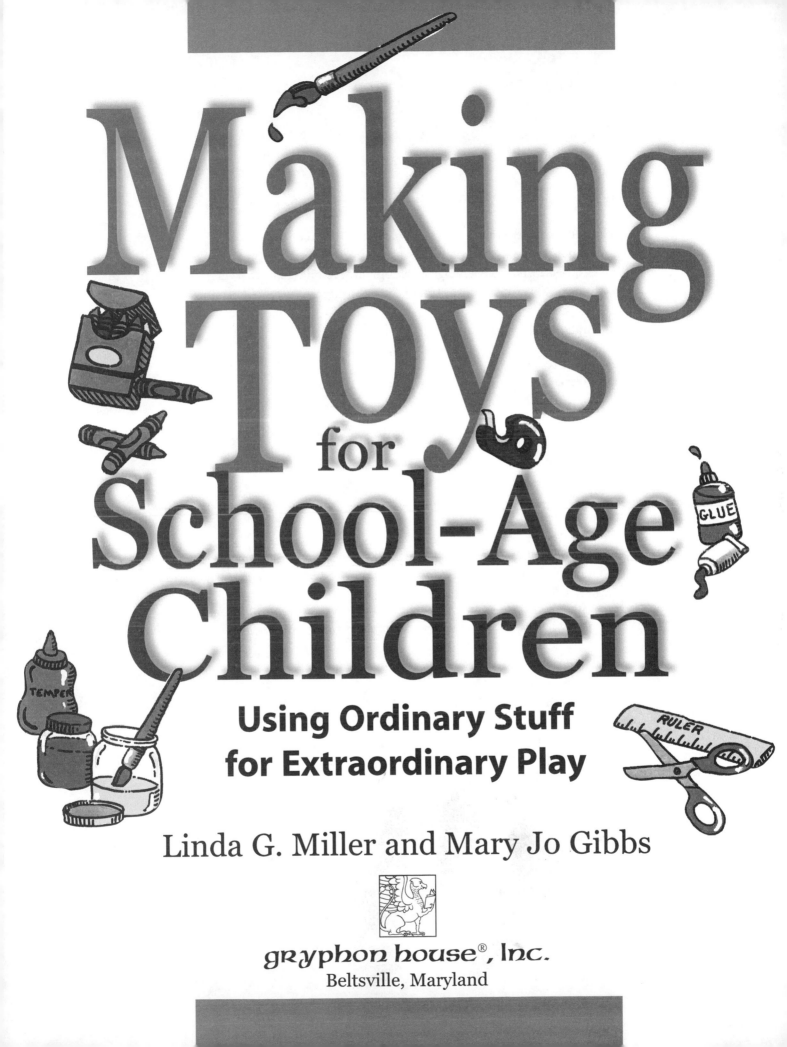

Making Toys
for
School-Age Children

**Using Ordinary Stuff
for Extraordinary Play**

Linda G. Miller and Mary Jo Gibbs

gryphon house®, Inc.
Beltsville, Maryland

Copyright

Published by Gryphon House, Inc.
10726 Tucker Street, Beltsville, MD 20705
301.595.9500; 301.595.0051 (fax); 800.638.0928

Visit us on the web at www.gryphonhouse.com

Illustrated by Kathy Dobbs

Library of Congress-Cataloging-in-Publication Data

Miller, Linda G.
  Making toys for school-age children : using ordinary stuff for extraordinary play / Linda G. Miller, Mary Jo Gibbs ; illustrated by Kathy Dobbs.
     p. cm.
Includes index.
 ISBN 0-87659-276-0
 1. Educational toys. 2. Educational games. 3. Early childhood education--Activity programs. I. Gibbs, Mary Jo, 1946- II. Dobbs, Kathy. III. Title.
 LB1029.T6 M55 2002
 371.33'7--dc21

                                                        2002007411

Bulk purchase

Gryphon House books are available at special discount when purchased in bulk. Special editions or book excerpts also can be created to specification. For details, contact the Director of Sales at the address or phone number on this page.

Disclaimer

The publisher and the authors cannot be held responsible for injury, mishap, or damages incurred during the use of or because of the activities in this book. The authors recommend appropriate and reasonable supervision at all times based on the age and capability of each child.

Table of Contents

Introduction

Teachers are creative, resourceful individuals. However, from time to time everyone needs fresh ideas. The experiences presented in this book are simple and inexpensive to create, so teachers can focus on interacting with the school-agers in their care. To determine what activities are appropriate, first observe the school-age children in your class to assess where they are developmentally and to determine their interests. Record what you observe using anecdotal notes, so you will have a record of progress.

Parents (and some teachers, too) often think that purchased materials are always superior to found or created items. However, teachers and school-agers can use everyday materials, such as boxes, gloves, mittens, socks, pantyhose, and bags to create high-quality learning materials. Always begin with items that are completely empty and clean. The key to using found and discarded items is being open to the limitless opportunities and the imagination of a school-age boy or girl.

Making Toys and Finding Materials

Teachers often find that everyday household materials and teacher-made or school-ager-made toys and materials are far more interesting than purchased learning materials and toys.

Consider the following guidelines for teacher-made toys:

- Make sure the toys and materials encourage action and/or interaction and help school-agers feel competent.
- Make multiple toys and learning materials. Share with other teachers or put the extras aside until you need them. Toys or learning materials made by teachers or school-agers may have a short life because of constant or rough use.
- Try to make open-ended toys that challenge school-agers on a variety of levels. That way you'll get more use out of what you do make.
- Check each homemade toy and learning material for safety. Check it again, and then ask another teacher to check it. Do not overlook safety issues in teacher-made toys. Get some help in insuring that the toys are safe.
- Begin with safe, clean materials.

Common household objects can make great toys or materials. Ideas for toys that you can make from common objects include:

- **Simple Hand Puppets**—Made from socks, mittens, or even small boxes, puppets are a good way to capture a school-ager's attention.
- **Boxes**—All shapes and sizes of boxes are appropriate for building, stacking, and putting things in. Very large boxes can make forts, playhouses, room dividers, set props, or even large costumes.
- **Sorting Toys**—A cardboard egg carton or a cupcake tin works well as a place to sort or store objects (for example, seeds, coins, and paperclips).
- **Dress-Ups**—School-agers enjoy putting on costumes, especially if there is a large mirror, so that they can see themselves. Costumes can be made from paper bags, cloth, or butcher paper. Use thread, yarn, staples, or tape to put costumes together. School-agers also enjoy presenting plays of all types, especially those they write themselves.
- **Books**—Use books throughout the classroom. School-agers love to write about themselves and experiences that they have together. Provide paper, writing materials, typewriters, and a computer, if possible. Parents will enjoy having a calendar of events or a school newsletter created by the school-agers.

The beauty of toys made by teachers and school-agers is that they are novel and interesting without costing much and can be discarded as they get used and worn out. New toys can be made to replace used ones, keeping the environment interesting and fun. Create lots of toys and materials in each zone.

Zones for School-Age Children

School-agers have different developmental needs and abilities than those of preschool children. For example, peer relationships are very important to school-age children. School-agers also have an increased ability to concentrate and are able to remain interested in an activity over a period of time. Therefore, the concept of zones instead of interest areas, which are used with preschool children, is appropriate for elementary school children. Zones are larger than interest areas, include more materials as choices, and allow school-agers to work together on larger and more complex projects.

Drama Zone—Younger school-agers may still enjoy traditional dramatic play with furniture sized to be appropriate for them. For most school-agers, however, the interest will be more in the area of real drama, including plays and narrative experiences. Because putting on a play (with school-agers or with puppets) involves so many different tasks, everyone can participate. Creating sets and background scenery, making costumes, writing the play, creating programs, designing invitations for parents, painting signs, helping actors learn lines, and acting are all exciting ways for school-agers to be involved.

Creative Construction Zone—School-agers enjoy building things—things that move, things that they can play with, things that show how creative they are. Activities in the creative construction zone include those that use traditional building materials, such as blocks, Legos, building logs, and straws. Some construction activities also can be very innovative, using items such as cartons, sheets of cardboard, and boxes. Be sure the children date and label their creations. Display these creations, so parents and classmates can see them. Create a full display for the classroom, and invite "patrons" to come and view the creations (as you would in a gallery exhibit).

Active Zone and Outside—School-agers enjoy exploring how their bodies move. A gym mat works well as a fall zone for trying out somersaults and cartwheels. Space may limit what you are able to provide in the classroom; however, many school-age programs have found that investing in a karoake machine is worthwhile for music and movement.

Outdoor time is an important part of the day for school-agers. The fresh air is a nice change from the closed environment of the classroom. Opportunities to be active—running, jumping, and being really—loud are needed after spending long periods of time being quiet indoors. Additionally, indoor activities that are moved outside take on new meaning. The sounds of the neighborhood, the way light changes because of clouds or shade, the feel of the breeze—all add to the richness of the outdoor experience. Outdoor experiences also provide a change of pace and variety for the teacher.

Creativity Zone—School-agers, like adults, are very interested in how an art activity turns out. They are striving for competency. Provide a mix of activities, including open-ended projects (true art) as well as those that are more step-by-step with parts or patterns (crafts). Ask the school-agers to date and write their names on all projects.

Display art where school-agers and their parents can see it. Save representative samples of art for portfolios. Also, consider creating a permanent art display (a trophy case in the foyer works well) to honor individual accomplishments.
For group projects, ask one of the school-agers to write about the process and/or take photographs of the process. Display the narrative and the pictures with the finished art projects. The narrative and photographs are especially important for large creations that are completed over a period of time (such as a backdrop for a stage).

In addition to traditional art supplies, provide unconventional and recycled items, such as plastic bottles, packing peanuts, paper of all types, computer parts, shells, rocks, boxes, cloth scraps, colored sand, polyester or cotton filler, magazines, junk mail, and sponges. School-agers can create amazing art creations with these interesting objects. Post a list of items you need, so parents can contribute (see page 135).

Games and Problem-Solving Zone—School-agers enjoy games with rules. Teach them to play card games such as Old Man/Maid, Go Fish, and even Hearts. Challenge school-agers to create their own card games. Use card stock, so they last longer. Board games (such as *Monopoly, Checkers*, and *The Game of Life*) are fun for school-agers. Provide materials, so school-agers can design their own games. Set up a structure for game tournaments and post a chart showing who has played and the results. Celebrate and crown the champions in a special event.

School-agers also enjoy honing their problem-solving skills by completing jigsaw puzzles. Their interest in puzzles can last for days (or even weeks) at a time. When a large puzzle is completed, help the students mount the puzzle on cardboard for a room decoration.

Problem-solving can take on many different forms. Brain-teasers, riddles, word problems, and "What would happen if . . . ?" challenges are all intriguing for school-agers. Also, help them develop estimation skills with activities such as "How many marbles fit inside a one-gallon jar?" or "How long would it take to walk the distance to the moon?"

Nature Zone—School-agers are fascinated by nature. Having animals and growing things in the classroom will help create a home-like atmosphere. Pets are also a great way to introduce science into the classroom. Always check licensing standards before introducing any animal. Nature Zone activities can be both inside and outside.

Themes, Special Events, and Holidays—Activities in this book can be used with a variety of themes and the special events or celebrations that are a natural part of a classroom. Take every opportunity to celebrate accomplishments of the group. Avoid celebrations (other than birthdays) that focus on one or only a few children. A similar caution exists for holiday celebrations. Allow children to share their own celebrations with classmates, instead of assuming that all children celebrate the same holidays. Also, be sensitive to children whose families do not celebrate holidays or other events, such as birthdays.

Teacher Tips—This section is filled with ideas that help teachers organize classroom materials, decorate classrooms, display student's work, create storage possibilities, and make simple games.

Projects

Projects are an effective way to keep school-agers interested and satisfied in what occurs in the classroom. Projects provide continuity across time and, at the same time, provide opportunities to perfect skills, to accomplish a goal, and to develop problem-solving skills. Post a set of very simple classroom rules (created by the school-agers) to facilitate projects in the classroom. After projects (such as an art gallery, an historical play, a gourmet cooking class, or a sports clinic) are completed, plan a time to celebrate everyone's accomplishments. Ask parents to share in the fun.

Group Time/Homeroom

Plan for two different group times or homeroom periods for school-agers. During group time or homeroom (in the morning), you can welcome children and set the tone for the day. Provide an overview of some of the activities they may choose and connect their prior learning to what they will be experiencing. During the afternoon, you can either connect what the school-agers did in the morning with afternoon experiences, or summarize the entire day and give a preview of what the next day will hold. Make group times short, and include such things as group reading and writing, charting experiences, making plans, and content-oriented activities.

How to Use This Book

The book includes eight sections:
- Drama Zone
- Creative Construction Zone
- Active Zone and Outside
- Creativity Zone
- Games and Problem-Solving Zone
- Nature Zone
- Themes, Special Events, and Holidays
- Teacher Tips

Following are some of the ways to use this book:
- First select an inexpensive material such as bags, boxes, socks, or gloves and then scan the table of contents or index to choose activities according to the material available.
- Choose activities based solely on the children's interests.
- Choose activities based on the main sections of the book.
- Provide a well-rounded, developmentally appropriate program for school-agers by selecting activities from each of the eight sections throughout the book.
- Use the book to get fresh ideas for a theme-based curriculum. Many activities are appropriate for a wide variety of themes.

Interpreting Each Activity

Each activity includes:
- Materials
- To Make
- To Use

Materials—includes all essential materials needed to complete the activity. Most activities use materials that are free, recycled, or very inexpensive. Additional materials are common arts and crafts supplies that are familiar and easily accessible to teachers. Always keep in mind safety precautions when using any material, especially if you substitute materials other than those listed. Closely supervise children, so they do not put dangerous items (such as plastic bags) into their mouths.

To Make—tells how to create the activity. This section provides step-by-step instructions for creating the learning material or toy. Many activities are illustrated to make the process even easier. School-agers will be able to make most of the toys with little or no help from adults. However, think about safety and be aware that some activities require the use of sharp or dangerous tools or materials, such as a craft knife, that should be used only by adults.

To Use—suggests ways to use the learning material or toy. However, teachers and children may find new ways to enjoy the learning material or toy. At all times, supervise school-agers and follow all safety precautions.

Drama Zone

Paper Bag Hats

Bags

Materials

large paper grocery bag

art supplies, such as paint, construction paper, scissors, markers,
   and so on

glue

To Make

- Fold down the opening of the bag two or three times. The fold
  eventually resembles a roll more than a fold.
- Keep folding (rolling) until the bag opening fits snugly onto the
  child's head.
- Punch down the square corners of the bag.
- Decorate the hat using art supplies.

To Use

- The hats are fun for celebrating holidays, as props for plays, or
  "Crazy Hat Day" creations.

Frog Mask

 Bags

Materials

paint
paintbrush
large paper bag
scissors
2 small paper cups
glue
black pompoms
party favor (the kind that rolls out when air is blown into it)

cut 2 paper
cups in half...

To Make

- Use paint to decorate the bag to look like frog skin.
- Cut out a large oval in the middle of one of the wide sides of the bag to make an opening for a child's face.
- Cut out half ovals from each narrow side of the bag at the opening (see illustration). These allow the bag to sit on a child's shoulders.
- Cut the two paper cups in half.
- Glue the bottom halves of the cups above the large oval for eyes.
- Glue black pompoms inside the cups to complete the eyes.

To Use

- Place the finished mask over the head, with the face showing through the oval cutout.
- Give each school-ager a personal party favor.
- The child blows the party favor to simulate a frog's tongue flicking out to catch an insect.
- These masks add an element of fun to the study of frogs, and they are great for dramatic play or for acting out songs.

Monster Costume

Bags

Materials

2 large grocery bags
scissors
2 paper cups
glue
black pompoms
butter knife

To Make

- To make the headpiece, start at the opening of one of the bags and cut 2" wide strips all the way around. Cut the strips to about 3" from the bottom of the bag.
- Cut two paper cups in half. Glue the bottoms of the cups near the bottom of the bag for eyes (see illustration).
- Glue a black pompom inside each cup to complete the eyes.
- Curl the strips by holding each strip on the blade of a butter knife and pulling the knife along the strip.
- To make the body, cut open the other paper bag to make a vest.
- Then, cut 2" wide strips from the opening of the bag down to the bottom of the bag.
- Use the butter knife to curl the strips (see illustration).

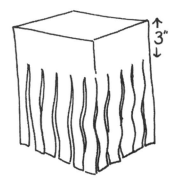

curl strips on a butter knife...

GLUE

To Use

- School-agers put on the vest and place the headpiece on their heads to role-play a monster.
- They may want to use the costume to act out stories or create a play.

Life-Size Puppets

 Bags

Materials

2 large grocery bags
scissors
art materials
construction paper
glue
pencil or marker
tape
hole punch
shoestring

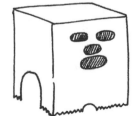

To Make

- Cut out large ovals from the narrow sides of the bag, so the bag fits over the head and rests on the shoulders (see illustration).
- Cut out holes for the eyes, nose, and mouth.
- Use art materials to decorate the face. Make construction paper hair or a hat and glue them in place.
- Cut off the wide sides from the second paper bag.
- Stack the two pieces of paper and trace around a hand to form a mitten shape.

- Tape the two pieces together to form each mitten.
- On the remaining paper, trace around a shoe to make two large feet.
- Use a hole punch to punch two holes in each foot. Thread a shoestring through the holes.

To Use

- School-agers tie the paper feet around their ankles, place the large mask over their heads, and put the large mittens on their hands to be a life-size puppet.

Mitt-Shaped Puppets

 Bags

Materials

large paper grocery bag
scissors
stapler
art supplies

To Make

- Cut off the wide sides from the grocery bag. Discard the bag and keep the two wide sides.
- Cut out a large half-oval in both pieces of paper.
- Staple the two shapes together, leaving the straight side open.
- Use art materials to decorate the puppet.

To Use

- School-agers may use these puppets for a show or make them into people or animal puppets to suit a theme.

Bag Mitt Puppets

 Bags

Materials
poster board
scissors
art materials
paper lunch bag
glue

To Make
- Cut out a front and a back of a puppet shape, such as people, animals, and so on, from poster board.
- Decorate the shapes with art supplies to make a front and back of a puppet.
- Glue the front of the puppet onto one side of the lunch bag, and glue the back of the puppet onto the other side of the bag.

To Use
- A school-ager places a hand inside the bag and makes the puppet move.

Lunch Bag Puppets

Bags

Materials
paper lunch bags
newspapers
toilet tissue tube
yarn
art supplies

To Make
- Stuff the bag with crumpled newspapers.
- Push a toilet tissue tube about halfway into the opening of the bag.

- Tie the opening securely closed with yarn.
- Turn the bag upside down and use art materials to create a face, hair, and decorations to hide the tied opening.

To Use
- School-agers hold the tube and make the puppet move as they read or tell stories.

Peanut Pals

 Bags

Materials
paper lunch bags
newspapers
tape
brown construction paper
scissors
glue
markers

To Make
- Stuff a lunch bag with crumpled newspaper.
- Tape the opening closed.
- Scrunch the middle of the bag to make it a peanut shape.

- Cut out strips of brown construction paper. To make vine-like arms and legs, accordion-fold the brown paper strips and glue them to the body.
- Cut out peanut-shaped feet and glue them to the ends of the legs.
- Use markers to draw a face on the top part of the bag.

To Use
- School-agers use the Peanut Pals as puppets.

Paper Bag Doll Puppet

Bags

Materials
large brown paper grocery bag
newspaper
string
paint
paintbrushes
poster board
scissors
glue
pantyhose

To Make
- Stuff the bottom of the bag with crumpled newspapers.
- Tie a string around the top part of the bag to make a head portion and to separate it from the body.
- Paint facial features on the head.
- Paint the other portion of the bag to look like a dress.
- Cut out arms and legs from poster board and paint it to match the face.
- When the paint is dry, glue the arms and legs in place on the bag.
- Cut off a leg from a pair of pantyhose. Cut it into strips and glue the strips onto the head for hair.

To Use

- To manipulate the puppet, place a hand inside the opening of the bag and grasp the inside of the bag.

Black Cat Bag Puppet

 Bags

Materials

paper lunch bag
black paint
paintbrush
white chalk
black construction paper
scissors
glue
gray or white yarn

To Make

- Paint a lunch bag using black paint.
- When the paint is dry, draw a white chalk cat face on the bottom of the bag.
- Cut out ears from black construction paper and glue them into place on the bag.
- Glue strands of white or gray yarn for whiskers.

To Use

- School-agers use the cat puppet to act out a story.

Brown Paper Bag Bear Puppet

 Bags

Materials
large brown paper bag
scissors
pencil
glue
markers
colored construction paper
newspaper

To Make
- Starting at a corner of the opening of the bag, make a vertical cut all the way down to the bottom of the bag.
- Then cut off the bottom of the bag, so that it makes a long flat sheet of paper.
- Crumple the paper many times to soften it. Then, flatten it out.
- Fold the paper in half and draw a bear shape on it.
- Hold the paper together and cut out two bear shapes.
- Glue the outside edges of the bear together, leaving the bottom open for a hand to fit through.
- After the edges are dried, draw on a nose, eyes, and a mouth.
- Decorate the bear with colored construction paper.
- Stuff crumpled newspaper into the head to add a little fullness.

To Use
- School-agers use the bear puppet to act out stories.

Octopus Puppet

Bags

Materials

paper lunch bag
paint and paintbrushes
plastic bottle
sand
newspaper
toilet tissue tube
rubber band or yarn
scissors
wiggle eyes
glue

To Make

- Open the brown paper bag and insert one forearm into it.
- With the other hand, paint the outside of the bag.
- Fill a plastic bottle with sand.
- Place the bag over the top of the plastic bottle to dry.
- When the paint is dry, crumple newspapers and stuff them into the bag. Fill only the bottom of the bag.
- Push a toilet tissue tube inside the bag.
- Use a rubber band or piece of yarn to seal the bag just above the newspaper stuffing to form the head of the octopus.
- Turn the bag upside down and cut the portion below the rubber band into eight sections for legs.
- Separate and twist each of the eight sections.
- Glue on wiggle eyes.

To Use

- School-agers use the octopus puppet as part of a theme-related activity or to tell stories.

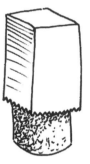

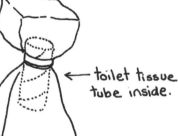

← toilet tissue tube inside.

Big Bag Animals

 Bags

Materials
large grocery bag
newspapers
tape
art supplies
paper plate
paint and paintbrushes
toilet paper and paper towel tubes
hole punch
pipe cleaners
scissors
poster board

To Make
- Stuff the grocery bag with folded newspapers that will lie flat inside the bag.
- Gather the opening of the bag and wrap tape around it to make a neck.
- Use art supplies to make an animal head on a paper plate.
- Tape the plate onto the neck at the top of the bag.
- Use paint to decorate the body of the desired animal.
- Use art materials to decorate the paper towel and toilet tissue rolls to make the animal's legs.
- Once decorated, punch a hole into opposite sides of the tissue rolls.
- Connect four sets (or as many sets as the animal has legs) of tissue rolls using pipe cleaners threaded through the holes.
- Use another pipe cleaner to attach each set of tissue rolls to the paper bag body to make legs.
- Cut out feet from poster board and glue them onto the ends of the legs.
- If the animal has a long tail, twist paper bags and tape them into place. Use a variety of art supplies to make other kinds tails (see illustration on p. 28).

To Use

■ This makes a large sculpture that can sit upright on a flat surface.

■ To make a puppet, cut a paper plate in half. Tape half of the paper plate on the back of the animal, leaving the straight edge of the plate open. The school-ager puts his hand underneath the plate to move the body. Attach a small dowel rod to one leg to move the leg.

■ This might work best as a partner puppet, with two school-agers necessary to move all the parts.

Cardboard Box Puppet Theater

 Boxes

Materials
very large cardboard box
duct tape
craft knife (adults only)
art materials
piece of fabric
string or yarn

To Make
- Remove any staples from the large box and cover any rough edges with duct tape.
- Away from the school-agers, use a craft knife to cut out a rectangular opening in the box near the top of one side (to make the puppet stage).
- Cut out another rectangular opening in the opposite side of the box near the bottom (so school-agers can get inside the puppet theater).
- Use art materials to decorate the box.
- If desired, use fabric, string or yarn, and duct tape to make a curtain for the puppet theater.

To Use
- Place the puppet theater in a carpeted area of the room, so the audience will have a comfortable area in which to sit.

Doll Bed

 Boxes

Materials

shoebox with lid
scissors
glue
paint or colored contact paper
fabric scrap

To Make

- Cut the lid of the shoebox in half horizontally.
- Discard one half of the lid.
- Glue the saved half to the inside of one end of the shoebox.
- Paint or cover the doll bed with colored contact paper.
- Cut a piece of fabric to fit inside the box as a blanket. Place it in the box.

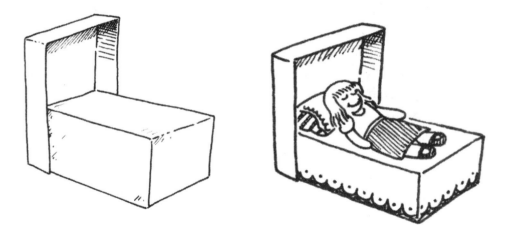

To Use

- Younger school-agers may use a small doll with the bed as part of dramatic play.

Bucket Space Helmets

 Boxes

Materials

fast food chicken buckets or large ice cream cartons
craft knife (adults only)
paper cups
glue
non-toxic silver spray paint (adults only)
pipe cleaners
pencil
tape

To Make

- Away from school-agers, use a craft knife to cut out a rectangular hole in the side of the bucket.
- With the school-agers, glue cups on the sides and on the top of the bucket.
- Away from school-agers and in a well-ventilated place, spray paint the bucket with non-tixic silver paint.
- With school-agers, wrap pipe cleaners around a pencil to make curly wires.
- Tape the curly stems on the helmet for antennas.

To Use

- School-agers wear the helmet as they role-play astronauts.

Cereal Box Suitcase

 Boxes

Materials

large cereal box
scissors
gift-wrap paper
tape
poster board
hole punch
2 paper fasteners
wide ribbon
hook and loop fastener, such as Velcro

To Make

- Cut across the top, down one side, and across the bottom of the front panel of the cereal box, making a lid for the suitcase.
- Cover the box with gift-wrap paper and tape it in place. Wrap the lid separately, so that it can open and close.
- Cut out a 2" wide strip of poster board, approximately 6" long.
- Punch a hole into each end of the strip.
- Punch two holes about 3" apart into the narrow side of the box and attach the poster board handle with two paper fasteners.
- Glue ribbon lengths around the suitcase on each end.
- Place hook and loop fasteners on the ends of the ribbon and to the side of the suitcase to hold the lid closed.

To Use

- Use the suitcase to hold art supplies, doll clothes, or a variety of collections.

Cardboard Box Airplane

 Boxes

Materials
large cardboard box
craft knife (adults only)
scissors
packing tape
poster board
aluminum foil
2 paper fasteners
paint
paintbrushes

To Make
- Away from the school-agers, use a craft knife to cut off the box flaps. Then cut out a large circular hole in the bottom of the box and cut out a three-sided flap on each of opposite sides.
- With school-agers, use one of the removed box flaps to cut out a windshield shape.
- Next, tape the windshield in front of the circular hole cut into the box.
- Cut out two propeller shapes from poster board.
- Cover the propeller blades with aluminum foil and attach them to the front of the airplane with paper fasteners.

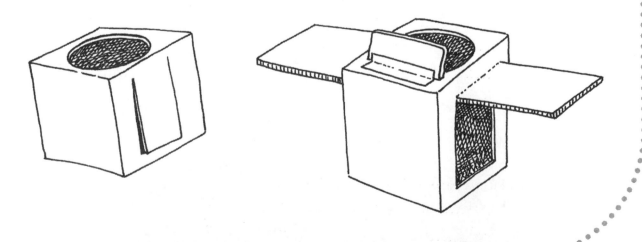

To Use

- The airplane goes on over the school-ager's body, with his head sticking out of the circular hole.
- To fly the airplane, he pushes his arms through the flaps on each side of the box to make wings.
- School-agers may design a logo and paint it on the airplane to create their own airline.

Cereal Box Bird Puppet

 Boxes

Materials

cereal box
newspapers
paper towel tube
tape
blue or red paint
paintbrushes
orange paint
2 shoulder pads
craft knife (adults only)
glue
2 buttons
craft feathers

To Make

- Stuff the cereal box with crumpled newspapers.
- Push a paper towel tube into the center of the box opening and tape it securely in place with the box flaps.

- Paint the box red or blue.
- Paint the shoulder pads orange.
- When the box is dry, away from the school-agers, use a craft knife to cut a slit into the center of one wide side of the box.
- With the school-agers, place the dry shoulder pads together to make a beak and push one end of the beak into the slit. Glue it into place.
- Glue buttons above the beak for eyes.
- Glue a few colored feathers at the top of the box.

cut a slit...

To Use

- School-agers hold the tube to make the bird puppet move.
- They may create a special voice, name, and personality for the puppet.

Autograph Glove Friend

 Gloves/Mittens

Materials
cotton gloves
fiberfill
needle and thread
permanent markers

To Make
- Stuff the glove with fiberfill.
- Sew the opening securely closed.
- Use permanent markers to draw facial features on the palm of the glove.

To Use
- School-agers name their glove friend and write the name somewhere on it.
- School-agers use permanent markers to autograph the glove friends.

Rubber Glove Puppets

 Gloves/Mittens

Materials
sticky dots
fine-tip marker
rubber dishwashing glove

To Make

- Draw funny faces on the sticky dots while they are still on the paper backing.
- Place the dots on each finger of the glove.

To Use

- School-agers place the glove on a hand and wiggle the fingers to make the puppets move.
- The individual characters might talk to each other or might be characters in a story.

Big Hands

 Gloves/Mittens

Materials

large-size work gloves
fiberfill
art materials, optional

To Make

- Stuff the gloves with fiberfill, leaving space to wiggle a child-size hand into the gloves.
- Decorate the gloves to reflect a particular costume or leave them plain.

To Use

- School-agers place their hands inside the gloves.
- They may wear the gloves with different costumes, such as clowns or animals, to give the illusion of big hands.

Glove and Plate Puppet

 Gloves/Mittens

Materials
glove
glue
sturdy paper plate
art supplies

To Make
- Glue a glove onto the bottom of a sturdy paper plate.
- Use art supplies to decorate the paper plate to make a person face, animal face, clown, or monster face.

To Use
- School-agers place a hand inside the glove to make the puppet move as they tell a story.

Storytelling Glove

 Gloves/Mittens

Materials
marker
felt
scissors
hook and loop fasteners, such as Velcro
cotton glove

To Make
- Trace or draw favorite story characters on pieces of felt.
- Cut out the character shapes.
- Attach hook and loop fasteners to the felt characters and to the glove.

To Use

■ School-agers use the felt characters and the glove to tell stories.

Mop Head Puppet

 Gloves/Mittens

Materials

gardening glove
glue
colorful yarn dust mop head
2 large wiggle eyes

To Make

■ Glue a gardening glove onto the back of a mop head.
■ Glue large wiggle eyes on the strings of the front of the mop head.

To Use

■ School-agers place a hand inside the glove and move the puppet.
■ School-agers may invent a special voice and personality for the puppet to use as they tell a story.

Mitten Rabbit

 Gloves/Mittens

Materials

white, black, and pink felt
scissors
glue
mitten
pink pompom or button

To Make

■ Cut out ears from white felt and glue them onto the back of the hand part of the mitten.

- Cut out eyes from black felt and glue them onto the mitten.
- Glue a pink pompom or button in place for the nose.

To Use

- School-agers use the puppet as they sing or tell a story.

Garden Glove Turtle Puppet

 Gloves/Mittens

Materials

green and brown felt
scissors
thick craft glue
brown jersey glove
cotton balls
wiggle eyes

To Make

- Cut out an oval from of a piece of green felt and glue it onto the back of the glove to make a turtle shell.
- Cut out brown felt "spots," and glue them on top of the green felt shell.
- Stuff one or two cotton balls into the middle finger of the glove for the head.
- Glue wiggle eyes onto the stuffed "turtle head."

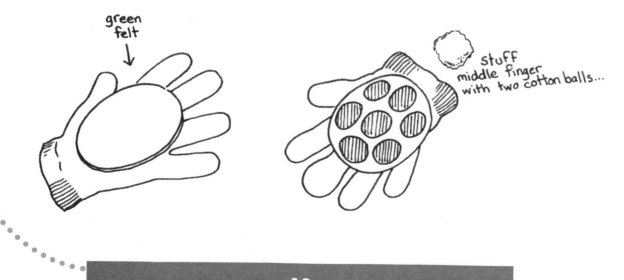

green felt

stuff middle finger with two cotton balls...

To Use

- School-agers place a hand inside the glove to make the puppet's head and legs.
- Use the puppet to present a puppet show, perhaps for younger children.

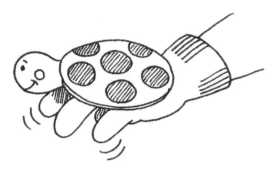

Mouse Puppets

 Gloves/Mittens

Materials

old glove
scissors
felt scraps
glue
yarn

To Make

- Cut off the fingers from the glove.
- Cut out ears, eyes, and a nose from felt scraps.
- Glue the facial features into place on the tip of the glove finger.
- Glue a short length of yarn at the opening of the finger for a tail.

To Use

- School-agers use the mouse puppet to act out a story or song.

Caterpillar Puppet

 Gloves/Mittens

Materials

old glove
scissors
green pompoms
glue
tiny wiggle eyes
sewing thread
black and colored felt
yarn
cotton ball

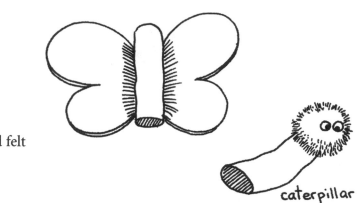

caterpillar

To Make

- Cut off two fingers from an old glove.
- On one finger, glue two or three green pompoms on one side.
- Glue tiny wiggle eyes onto the first pompom to make a caterpillar face. Glue sewing thread on the fingertip for antennae.
- Decorate the second finger to be a butterfly, using black felt for the body and colored felt for the wings. Glue yarn to one side for the antennae. Glue tiny wiggle eyes onto the butterfly.

To Use

- School-agers may want to use these two finger puppets and a cotton ball cocoon to demonstrate the life cycle of a butterfly.

Pantyhose Wig

 Socks/Pantyhose

Materials

3 pairs of pantyhose
scissors
yarn

To Make

- Cut off the leg portions from two pairs of old, clean pantyhose.
- Tie the two legs to each leg of a third pair of clean, old pantyhose.
- Braid each leg and tie the ends with yarn to make pigtails.

To Use

- School-agers place the panty portion of the pantyhose on their head to wear this wig with pigtails.

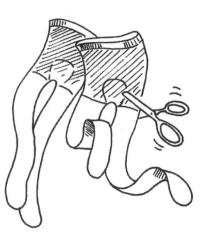

Pantyhose Masks

 Socks/Pantyhose

Materials

wire coat hangers
pantyhose
scissors
duct tape
paint
paint brushes
art materials

To Make

- Bend the wire coat hangers into a desired shape, twisting the hook portion into a handle.
- Cut off part of one of the legs of the pantyhose.
- Stretch this piece of pantyhose over the wire frame and secure it with duct tape.
- Cover any sharp edges of the coat hanger with layers of duct tape.
- Cut out openings for eyes, a nose, and a mouth in the mask.
- Use paint and other art materials to decorate the mask.

← cover handle with duct tape.

To Use

- School-agers use the mask to act out stories.

Sock Caterpillar

 Socks/Pantyhose

Materials

child-sized white sock
fiberfill
yellow paint or yellow sock
paintbrushes
green paint or green contact paper
paper towel tube
scissors
glue
pipe cleaner
wiggle eyes

To Make

- Stuff the sock with fiberfill to make a caterpillar body.
- Tuck the open end of the sock down into itself on one side to close the sock and form a mouth for the caterpillar.

- Paint the sock body yellow (or just use a yellow sock).
- Paint the paper towel tube green or cover it with green contact paper.
- Allow the paint to dry.
- Cut the paper towel tube into four wide rings.
- Slide the rings over the body of the caterpillar and arrange them so they are evenly spaced to give the caterpillar stripes.
- Glue the rings in place.
- Cut a 4" piece of pipe cleaner.
- Thread one end of the pipe cleaner into one side of the top of the head and out the other to make antennae.
- Bend the ends of the pipe cleaner to the side.
- Glue two wiggle eyes to the front of the caterpillar, above the mouth.

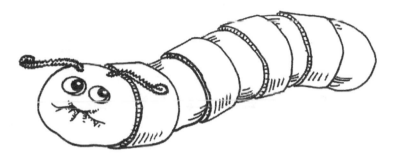

To Use

- School-agers use the caterpillar as a puppet to act out a story.

Pop-Up Dog Puppet

 Socks/Pantyhose

Materials

small round oatmeal container
scissors
adult-size brown sock
12" dowel
glue
2 ½" Styrofoam ball
string/yarn
2 wiggle eyes
brown felt scraps

To Make

- Cut off the bottom of the oatmeal container.
- Slide the sock over the box, so that the cuff opening of the sock just fits around the edge of the container.
- The container will be the dog's house.
- Dip one end of the dowel into glue, and then push it into the Styrofoam ball.
- Push the ball through the container and into the toe of the sock, with the dowel coming out of the bottom of the box.
- The ball will be the head of the dog.
- Tie a piece of string around the stick at the base of the ball to make the dog's neck.
- Glue the two wiggle eyes on one side of the dog's head.
- Cut out ears and a nose from brown felt and glue them into place.

remove the bottom...

stretch the sock over the box

To Use

- Push on the stick to make the dog pop out of his house. Use the puppet to tell stories.

Pop Up Pup!!

Scarecrow Puppet

 Socks/Pantyhose

Materials

old white sock
scissors
yellow yarn
14" stick
2 or more old neckties
10" stick
glue
felt and fabric scraps
2 buttons
yellow cupcake liner

To Make

- Cut off a 4" piece from the toe end of the sock.
- Cut the rest of the sock into small pieces and stuff them into the cut-out toe end. This is the head of the scarecrow.
- Use a piece of yarn to tie the stuffed head closed around one end of the 14" stick.
- Cut a 12" long rectangle from the wide end of a necktie.
- Fold the rectangle in half and cut a small slit in the center of the fold for a neck hole.
- Put the bottom end of the stick down through the neck hole in the necktie.
- Then, slide the tie piece up under the head of the scarecrow to make the body.
- Cut out a 10" strip from the thin end of a necktie for arms.
- Cut the ends of the tie into points.
- Slide the 10" stick through the tie arms to support them.
- Glue the arms between the front and back of the body, so that they stick out on each side of the scarecrow.
- Cut out a 12" piece from the thin end of another necktie. Trim the points.
- Fold the piece in the center to make a "V" shape.
- Glue the point of the "V" shape between the bottom of the front and back of the body, so that the two ends hang down to form two legs for the scarecrow.
- Glue yellow yarn for straw at the neck, hands, and feet of the scarecrow.

- Glue the two buttons on the head for eyes.
- Cut out a triangle from felt to make a nose and glue it in place.
- Glue the yellow cupcake liner on the scarecrow's head for a hat.

① ← 4" →

② stuff the toe end with cut up bits from the remaining sock.

③ 14" stick

④ 12"

⑤ neck hole

⑥ slide up for the body.

10"

cut the ends of the 10" strip into points.

slide 10" stick inside tube.

To Use

- Hold the stick to make the puppet move as you sing, read, or tell a story.

Creative Construction Zone

Star Box

 Boxes

Materials
shoebox
black paint
paintbrush
golf tee
plastic hammer
flashlight

To Make
- Paint the outside bottom of the shoebox black.
- Use a golf tee and a plastic hammer to make holes in the bottom of the box to represent real or created constellations. (Consult a book on constellations to get patterns.)

To Use
- Darken the room and shine a flashlight into the open end of the box, so the light will shine through the holes to reveal the star patterns.
- Make several Star Boxes and put on a constellation show.

Box Creatures

 Boxes

Materials
different sizes of cardboard boxes (such as tissue, cereal, and other food)
duct tape
paint
paintbrushes
art supplies

To Make
- Tape a variety of boxes together to make a creature shape.
- Use paint and art supplies to create unique creatures.

To Use
- Display the creature sculptures in an art show or museum. Label each creation with the artist's name and the date it was created.

Animal Poles

 Boxes

Materials
cardboard boxes
paint
paintbrushes
art supplies
glue
tape
black marker

To Make
- Paint each box to represent an animal.
- Glue a variety of art supplies (such as feathers, felt scraps, and buttons) to the box to complete the animal.
- Stack the box animals on top of each other to form a pole.
- Secure the boxes in place with tape.
- Paint the boxes with brown paint and draw wood grain to make the totem pole look like carved wood.

To Use
- Display as part of an animal theme.

Match Box Car Races

 Boxes

Materials

toy cars
large pieces of heavy cardboard
permanent markers
notebook or chart
pencils or pens

To Make

- Collect toy cars (ask parents and school-agers to bring them in). They are also readily available at garage sales.
- Make tracks for the car races using large pieces of heavy cardboard. The tracks must be long enough to span the distance from the edge of a table to the floor.
- Tracks will need to be straight from one end of the board to the opposite end.
- Decorate the pieces of cardboard using permanent markers.

To Use

- School-agers can race cars in teams or individually.
- Keep the race results in a notebook or on a chart posted in the classroom.
- The school-agers can add weights (such as coins) to the cars to increase their speed.
- Encourage them to change cars from one day to the next.

Little Box Vehicles

 Boxes

Materials
variety of small boxes (toothpaste box, match box, jewelry gift boxes, small food boxes, and so on)
glue
buttons or plastic bottle caps
art supplies
paint
paintbrushes

To Make
- Glue small boxes together in creative ways to make replicas of real or make-believe vehicles.
- Glue buttons or plastic bottle caps onto the boxes for wheels.
- Use art materials and paint to complete the vehicles.

To Use
- School-agers name their vehicles, write stories about them, and set up a display.

Box City

 Boxes

Materials
variety of sizes and shapes of cardboard food boxes
newspapers
tape
paint
paintbrushes
art supplies
construction paper
scissors
glue
toy vehicles

To Make

- Stuff each box with crumpled newspapers and tape the opening securely closed.
- Use paint and art supplies to make the boxes into houses, businesses, and community buildings. Make streets out of construction paper.

To Use

- Set up the buildings into a community along the construction paper streets.
- School-agers roll small toy vehicles along the streets.

Variation

- Help school-agers create a map of the neighborhood. Then create the box city using the map as the pattern.

Water Wheel

 Boxes

Materials

cylindrical oatmeal container
craft knife (adults only)
dowel or unsharpened pencil
water faucet

To Make

- Away from the school-agers, use a craft knife to cut the oatmeal container in half horizontally.
- Remove the lid and put it on the bottom half of the box.
- Discard the top half.
- Cut six flaps around the middle of the cylinder and bend them back, so the holes are open.
- Cut a hole in the top and bottom of the cylinder, and push a dowel or pencil through them.

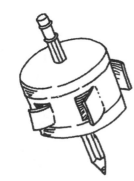

To Use

- Turn on a faucet.
- School-agers hold onto the dowel stick with both hands and position the flaps on the cylinder under the running water, so that the water wheel spins.

Variation

- Try different shapes (such as juice cans, cardboard tubes, and salt boxes). Water wheels will last longer if you spray paint them with gloss paint (away from the school-agers).

Milk Carton Barge

 Boxes

Materials

half-gallon milk carton
craft knife (adults only)
tape
hole punch
string

To Make

- Away from the school-agers, use a craft knife to cut the clean milk carton in half from the top to the bottom.
- With the school-agers, tape the opening of one half of the carton securely in place.
- Punch a hole in the top of the carton and tie a length of string through the hole.

To Use

- School-agers pull the string to move the "barge" through water.
- Experiment with a variety of materials to see how much the barge can carry without sinking.

Milk Carton Rowboat

 Boxes

Materials

pint-size milk carton
craft knife (adults only)
tape
scissors
2 craft sticks
liquid soap
dark paint
paintbrush

To Make

- Away from the school-agers, use a craft knife to cut the clean milk carton in half from the top to the bottom.
- With school-agers, tape the opening flaps together.
- Cut off a 2" wide section from one of the carton pieces.
- Fold the piece to look like a bench. Tape it inside the square end of the other carton piece to make a bench for the rowboat.
- Cut a slit into each long side of the milk carton. Push a craft stick through each slit for oars.
- Put a few drops of liquid soap into dark paint, so the paint will adhere to the waxed carton.
- Apply one or two coats of paint to cover the print on the carton.

cut milk carton in half.

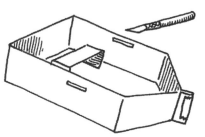

To Use

- School-agers place the boat in water and move it around with the oars.

Variations

- Create a sail with paper and craft sticks. Attach the sail to the boat using tape.
- Race boats outside in a shallow wading pool.

Active Zone and Outside

Emergency Kickball

Bags

Materials
paper grocery bags
newspapers
tape

To Make
- Place one paper bag inside of another paper bag.
- Fill the bag with crumpled newspapers, and then tape the opening securely closed.
- Punch and shape the bag to make a large ball shape.

To Use
- School-agers can use the ball for a kickball, volleyball, or basketball (with a large box as the "basket").

Paddle Ball

Bags

Materials
two wire coat hangers
duct tape
two mesh produce bags
pantyhose
scissors
fiberfill

To Make
- Bend the hangers into diamond shapes and twist the hooks into a handle.
- Cover the handles with duct tape to cover any sharp ends.
- Make two paddles by stretching the mesh produce bags over each metal frame. Securely tape the bags in place.
- Cut off a 12" length of pantyhose.

- Stuff fiberfill into the pantyhose length and tie a knot in the end.
- Shape the pantyhose into a ball.

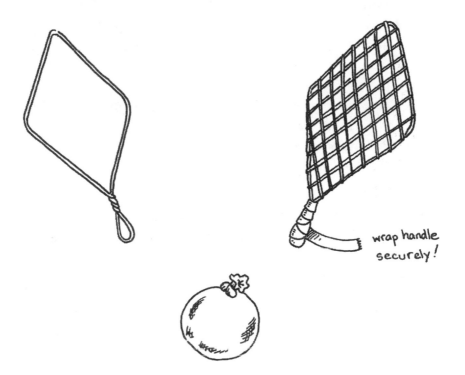

wrap handle securely!

To Use
- School-agers bat the ball back and forth using the paddles.

Plastic Bag Parachute

 Bags

Materials
pipe cleaner
plastic bread or produce bag
ruler
string
scissors

To Make

- Bend the pipe cleaner into the shape of a person to make a skydiver.
- Using a ruler, measure 5" up from the bottom of the plastic bag.
- Cut off the top of the bag above the 5" mark. Discard the top part.
- Cut two 12" pieces of string.
- Gather the bottom part of the bag into two different corners.
- Tie a piece of string to each corner.
- Wind the other end of the string to an arm of the skydiver.
- Bend the skydiver's hands over the string to hold it securely in place.

To Use

- Toss the skydiver in the air, and watch the parachute open and break the skydiver's fall.

Flying Fish Kite

Bags

Materials

brown paper bag
scissors
string
glue
paint
paintbrush
24" dowel stick

To Make

- Cut off the bottom of a paper bag.
- Cut along one side of the bag from top to bottom to make a large sheet of brown paper.
- Fold under 1" along one side of the bag and place a piece of string underneath the fold, allowing 24" of string to hang free on one side.
- Glue the fold over the string.
- Glue the two short ends of the paper together to form a cylinder, with the string hanging from the top.
- Cut out fins from another paper bag and glue them onto the fish body.
- Paint on eyes, scales, gills, and a tail.
- Tie the string on the fish to the dowel stick.

24' of string hanging free..

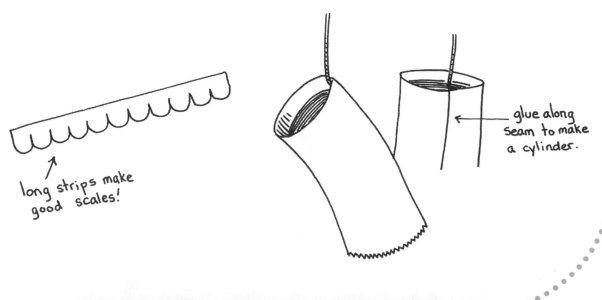

long strips make good scales!

glue along seam to make a cylinder.

To Use

- School-agers hold the dowel stick and wave the fish in the air.

Dice Baseball

 Boxes

Materials

cube-shaped cardboard box
tape
craft paper
markers
poster board
chalkboard and chalk
four chairs

To Make

- Tape the cardboard box securely closed.
- Cover the box with craft paper and tape it in place.
- Use a marker to make dots on each side of the box to make a die.

- Write the baseball value for each roll of the die on a piece of poster board.
- The baseball value for each roll of the die is: 1 = single, 2 = double, 3 = triple, 4 = homerun, 5 = out, and 6 = out.

To Use

- Divide the children into two teams. Designate a scorekeeper to keep score on a chalkboard.
- Place four chairs in a diamond shape to represent home plate, first, second, and third bases.
- Each batting team gets three outs before giving up the die to the other team.
- The batter tosses the die onto the floor in front of the home plate chair.
- After the batter rolls the die, she moves to the appropriate base or scores an out for the team. For example, if she rolls a "2," she moves to second base.
- Play progresses like baseball with the players staying on base until the roll of the die moves them the appropriate spaces.
- The scorekeeper uses hash marks to indicate each player crossing the home plate.
- Each batter gets only one roll of the die per turn.
- When three outs are rolled, the teams trade places.
- At the end of nine innings, the team with the highest score wins.
- The game may be played inside or outside.

Broom Ball

 Boxes

Materials

large cardboard box
craft knife (adults only)
brooms
lightweight ball

To Make

- Away from the school-agers, use a craft knife to cut out a tunnel-shaped hole in the wide side of a large cardboard box.
- Place the box on the ground with the tunnel facing the school-agers.

To Use

- The school-agers use the brooms to "sweep" the ball into the box, working either individually or in teams.

Bucket Golf

 Boxes

Materials

fast food chicken buckets or large ice cream cartons
craft knife (adults only)
spray paint (adults only)
golf clubs
plastic golf balls

To Make

- Away from the school-agers, use a craft knife to cut out a tunnel-shaped hole into each bucket.
- Away from the school-agers and in a well-ventilated area, spray paint the buckets with bright colors.

To Use

- Place the buckets in a pattern around the playground.
- School-agers use the golf clubs to putt the balls into the buckets.

Milk Carton Catch

 Boxes

Materials
quart-size milk carton
craft knife (adults only)
liquid soap
tempera paint
paintbrushes
art materials
tennis ball

To Make
- Away from the school-agers, use a craft knife to cut off the top of the milk carton, leaving the straight sides.
- With the school-agers, add a few drops of liquid soap to the tempera paint to help the paint stick to the waxed carton.
- Paint the milk carton and use art materials to decorate the carton.

To Use
- School-agers toss a tennis ball and catch it with the carton.

Soft Horseshoes

 Gloves/Mittens

Materials
mittens
dry beans
needle and thread
hoops

To Make
- Fill mittens with dry beans and sew the opening securely closed.

To Use

- Place hoops on the floor, about 10' apart.
- Younger school-agers can take turns tossing the mittens into the hoops.
- Older school-agers may want to use smaller hoops, make up rules, and keep score.

Sock Balls

 Socks/Pantyhose

Materials

large socks

To Make

- Roll socks together into a ball shape.
- Tuck the ends of the sock inside the opening.

To Use

- Sock balls are fun for throwing, catching, playing ball games, or tossing at targets.
- Balls may be used inside or outside.

Pantyhose Balls

 Socks/Pantyhose

Materials

pantyhose
scissors
fiberfill

To Make

- Cut pantyhose into 12" lengths.
- Tie a knot in one open end of the hose and turn it inside out, putting the knot on the inside.
- Fill the hose with fiberfill and shape it into a ball. Tie a knot to close the opening.

To Use

- These soft balls are easy to wash and dry, and are great for throwing and tossing games.

Variation

- Fill the panty portion of the pantyhose with fiberfill to make a giant ball that can be used for tossing into a box or through a hoop.

Pantyhose Bats

 Socks/Pantyhose

Materials

wire clothes hangers
duct tape
pantyhose
scissors

To Make

- Bend the wire coat hangers into a bat shape.
- Twist the hook portions into a tight handle.
- Wrap layers of duct tape around the handles to cover any sharp edges.
- Cut off the legs of pantyhose.
- Stretch a pantyhose leg over each wire shape and secure any leftover hose with duct tape around the handle.

To Use

- School-agers use the bats with pantyhose balls for playing alone or with a friend.

Toss and Catch

Socks/Pantyhose

Materials
pantyhose
scissors
fiberfill
craft knife (adults only)
large plastic jug with a handle
yarn

To Make
- Cut off a 12" length from a pair of pantyhose.
- Stuff the pantyhose length with fiberfill and knot the ends to make a ball.
- Away from the school-agers, use a craft knife to cut off the bottom of a large plastic jug with a handle.
- With the school-agers, tie a piece of yarn to the pantyhose ball and tape the other end of the yarn to the inside of the jug.

To Use
- School-agers hold the jug by the handle, swing the ball up in the air, and catch it in the jug.

use a craft knife to remove bottom of a plastic jug...

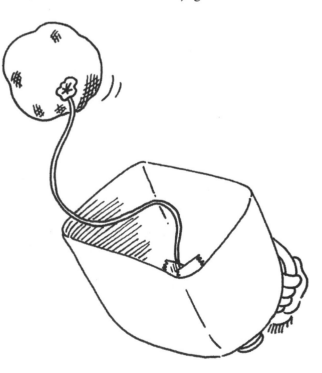

Creativity
Zone

Grocery Bag Art Books

 Bags

Materials
brown paper grocery bags
scissors
hole punch
book rings
crayons or markers

To Make
- Cut off the wide sides of brown paper grocery bags.
- Punch holes into one side of the pages and fasten them together with book rings.

To Use
- School-agers draw pictures on the pages and write or dictate stories to go with the pictures.

Paper Bag Blank Books

 Bags

Materials
6 brown paper grocery bags
scissors
glue
hole punch
yarn, pipe cleaners, or book rings

To Make

- Cut off the bottoms of all six bags, slit them open, and lay them flat.
- Spread glue on one sheet and place another sheet on top of it, making a double sheet. Do this with all of the bags to make three double sheets.
- Stack the three sheets together, fold them in half, and use a hole punch to make holes along the left side at the top, middle, and bottom.
- Use yarn, pipe cleaners, or silver book rings to hold the book together.

To Use

- School-agers use the blank books to create their own books.

Paper Bag Piñatas

Bags

Materials

colored tissue paper
glue
brown paper grocery bags
confetti
yarn
cardboard gift-wrap tubes

To Make

- Crumple pieces of tissue paper and glue them onto the outside of the bag, covering the whole bag.
- Fill the bag with confetti, and then twist the opening of the bag closed.
- Tie the opening securely closed with yarn, leaving enough yarn to hang the piñata from the ceiling.

To Use

- School-agers take turns hitting the piñata with long cardboard gift-wrap tubes.
- The object is to break open the piñata and spill the confetti.

Coloring Bags

Bags

Materials
rubbing alcohol (adult supervision needed)
measuring cup
zipper-closure plastic bags
food coloring
rice or sand
paper towels

To Make
- Measure ½ cup rubbing alcohol into a zipper-closure plastic bag.
- Add drops of food color until the desired shade is reached.
- Pour rice or sand into the bag.
- Seal the bag and shake it until the rice or sand is thoroughly covered with color.
- Place the colored rice or sand on layers of paper towels to dry.

Note: Adult supervision at all times is essential for this activity.

To Use
- Colored rice or sand may be used for art projects or sensory experiences.

Paper Bag Sculptures

 Bags

Materials
plaster of Paris
water
bowl
spoon
paper lunch bag
paint
paintbrushes
art materials

To Make

- Mix water and plaster of Paris in a bowl according to the directions on the package.
- Pour the mixture into a paper bag.
- Squeeze the bag to shape the soft plaster into a desired shape.
- Allow the plaster to harden.
- Tear off the paper from the plaster shape.
- Use paints or other art materials to decorate the plaster shape.

To Use

- Sculptures might be a part of an art gallery of school-agers' creations.

Decorated Bags

Bags

Materials

brown paper grocery bags
glue
paint
paintbrush
art supplies
stapler

To Make

- Fold down 8" of the top of the large bag.
- Glue the fold into place on the inside of the bag.
- Paint the outside of the bag or decorate it with various art supplies.
- Twist another bag into a handle, 20" long, and staple it into place on the narrow sides of the bag.

To Use

- Use the bags for decorations or for wrapping gifts.

Flower Bags

Bags

Materials

paper lunch bags
art supplies
colored tissue paper
scissors
green construction paper
glue
ribbon

To Make

- Use art supplies to decorate a paper lunch bag.
- Cut out 4" circles from colored tissue paper.
- Place two or three tissue paper circles on top of each other.
- Pinch the stack of circles in the center to make a flower shape.
- Cut out stems and leaves from green construction paper and glue them to the flowers.
- Fold over the opening of the bag two or three times.
- Place the flowers inside the bag.
- Squeeze the bag closed and secure it under the fold with a ribbon bow.

To Use

- Use the Flower Bags for table decorations or gifts.

Paper Bag Dragon

 Bags

Materials
brown paper grocery bag
scissors
crepe paper streamers
tape
crayons or markers

To Make
- Cut out an oval from the narrow sides of a large grocery bag to fit the shoulders of a child.
- Depending upon the age and ability of the child, cut out eyeholes or a face-size hole in a wide side of the bag.
- Tape colorful crepe paper streamers around the bag.
- Use crayons or markers to decorate bag.

To Use
- School-agers place the dragon mask over their heads to act out Chinese New Year celebrations or plays, songs, or rhymes about dragons.

Place-Mats

 Bags

Materials
brown paper grocery bags
scissors
decorations (such as real leaves, paper die cuts, and fabric scraps)
glue
paint and paintbrushes, optional
clear contact paper

To Make
- Cut down the seam of one side of the large paper bag and cut off the bottom to make one large piece of paper.
- Cut out two 14" x 10" sheets.
- Glue one sheet on top of the other.
- Fold over the edges 1" on all sides and glue in place.
- Paint the mat or leave it natural.
- Glue decoration items in place.
- After the glue dries, cover the entire mat with clear contact paper.

To Use
- Use these place-mats to set the table or for special event decorations.

"Leather" Animals

Bags

Materials
brown paper grocery bags
scissors
stapler
old newspapers
crayons or markers

To Make

- Cut down the seam on one side of the large paper bag and cut off the bottom to make one large piece of paper.
- Cut out two identical animal shapes from the brown paper.
- Crumple the animal shapes into a ball and then smooth them out again to give them the texture of leather.
- Staple the two shapes together, leaving an opening on one side.
- Stuff crumpled newspapers inside the shape, and then finish stapling the opening closed.
- Use crayons or markers to decorate the shape.

To Use

- Place animal shapes in a museum display (each labeled with artist's name and date created) or hang them from the ceiling to decorate.

Plastic Bag Butterfly

 Bags

Materials

wooden clamp clothespin
yellow paint
paintbrush
colored tissue paper scraps, aluminum foil pieces, or confetti
gallon-size, zipper-closure plastic bag
pipe cleaner
glue
two wiggle eyes
sticky-back magnetic strip

To Make

- Paint the clothespin yellow and allow it to dry.
- Fill the plastic bag lightly with colorful bits of tissue paper, confetti, or foil pieces.
- Seal the bag closed.
- Gather the bag together at the center, and slide it between the clamps of the clothespin.
- Shape the ends of the pipe cleaner into antennae and glue the pipe cleaner between the clamps of the clothespin.

- Glue wiggle eyes onto one flat side of the clothespin.
- Press a piece of sticky-back magnetic strip onto the side of the clothespin opposite the eyes.

To Use
- Use the butterfly as a decoration or a note holder on a metal surface.

Brown Bag Note Cards

 Bags

Materials
2 brown paper grocery bags
scissors
envelopes
pencil
glue
fancy-edge scissors
small leaves
green and brown crayons
stickers

To Make

- Cut down the seam of one side of the large paper bag and cut off the bottom to make one large piece of paper.
- Carefully unglue the seams of an envelope and spread it out flat to use as a pattern.
- Trace around the envelope onto the grocery bag paper.
- Cut out the outline.
- Fold the brown paper envelope shape at exactly the same places as the original envelope.
- Glue the seams together, leaving the top open.
- Use fancy-edge scissors to cut out a rectangle from brown paper that is the same width as the envelope.
- Fold the rectangle in half to make a note card.
- To decorate the note card, place two or three leaves between the fold of the note card.
- Rub brown and green crayons over the top of the paper to make rubbings of the leaves.

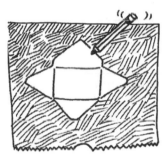 

To Use

- School-agers write or dictate a note on the inside of the card, place it inside the matching envelope, and seal it with a sticker.
- Experiment with different techniques.
- The envelope and note card set make great gifts or fundraisers.

Box Collage

 Boxes

Materials

cardboard boxes in a variety of sizes
newspapers
hole punch
tape
art supplies (such as feathers, buttons, ribbon, pompoms, colored
   tissue paper, gift-wrap, felt scraps, and stickers)
glue
nylon fishing line

To Make

- Fill a box with crumpled newspaper.
- Punch a hole into each end of two box flaps.
- Close the box using the two flaps without holes. Tape it securely closed.
- Glue a variety of materials to all sides of the box.
- When the glue has dried, thread fishing line through the holes in the flaps and secure with knots.

To Use

- Thread a length of fishing line through the two box flaps that have holes and hang the boxes from the ceiling for a hanging display.

Photo Collage

 Boxes

Materials
photos and/or pictures from magazines
scissors
cardboard box
glue
felt-tip pen
clear contact paper

To Make
- Choose a variety of photos or a cut out a collection of interesting pictures from magazines.
- Glue the pictures onto a cardboard box in an interesting collage.
- Use a felt-tip pen to label the pictures, or write stories on the box.
- Cover the entire box with clear contact paper.

To Use
- Display photos from a special event or field trip, or showcase pictures that are theme- or interest-related.

Cardboard Box Lacing

 Boxes

Materials
milk carton
craft knife (adults only)
hole punch
tape
yarn

To Make

- Away from the school-agers, use a craft knife to cut off the top of the milk carton.
- With the school-agers, use a hole punch to make rows of holes, evenly spaced, from the top of the carton to the bottom.
- Wrap tape around the ends of yarn to make a "needle."

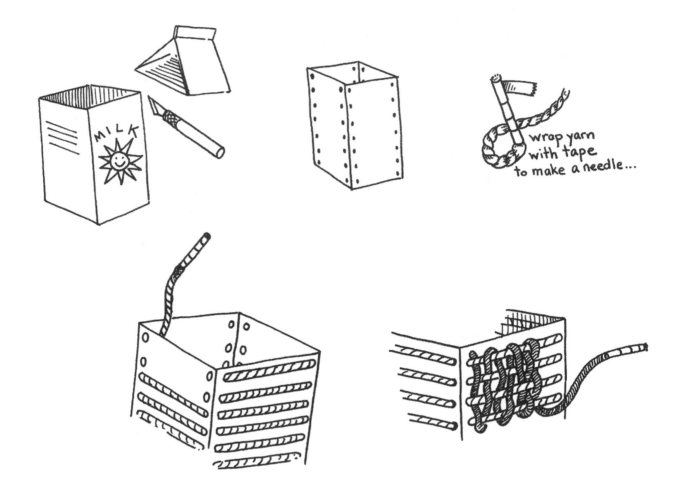

To Use

- Weave the yarn in and out of the holes in the milk carton to cover the box with yarn.
- One color or many colors of yarn may be used to create woven designs.

Gardening Glove Plant Pal

 Gloves/Mittens

Materials
gardening gloves
permanent markers
dimensional fabric paint
small gardening tools

To Make
- Use permanent markers and dimensional fabric paint to decorate the gardening gloves.

To Use
- When completed, slip small, hand gardening tools into the open ends of the gloves. Attach the gloves near the potting area to keep tools handy.

Hand Painters

 Gloves/Mittens

Materials
textured materials, such as a net scrub sponge, powder puff, length of lace, nylon bath sponge, terry cloth, or piece of bubble wrap
scissors
mittens
glue
paint
shallow pans
paper

To Make

- Cut out pieces of textured materials to fit in the palm of a mitten.
- Glue a different texture to each mitten.
- Pour paint into shallow pans.

To Use

- School-agers place the mitten of choice on one hand.
- They carefully dip the textured part of the mitten into paint and make prints on paper.
- They may enjoy experimenting with different types of paper, such as tissue paper, brown paper bags, slick shelf-lining paper, or even sandpaper.

Collage Glove Sun Catchers

 Gloves/Mittens

Materials

plastic food service gloves
shiny, colorful art materials (such as glitter, sequins, spangles, colored plastic report covers, and colored cellophane)
glue
string
clothespins

To Make

- Glue each piece of the shiny art material on the inside of a food service glove, taking time to glue the materials facing out on both sides of the glove.
- When the desired collage is completed, glue the opening of the glove securely closed.
- Attach the gloves to lengths of string using clothespins.

To Use

- Hang the gloves in a sunny widow or outside to pick up the sunlight.

Garden Glove Windsocks

 Gloves/Mittens

Materials

jingle bells
ribbons
cotton gardening gloves
needle and thread
twine
dimensional fabric paint

To Make

- Thread jingle bells onto the ends of ribbons and tie them securely in place.
- Sew the ribbons onto the fingertips of a glove.
- Sew each end of twine to each side of the inside cuff of the glove to form a loop.
- Use dimensional fabric paint to decorate the hand portion of the glove.

To Use

- Hang the windsocks where breezes will make them move and jingle.

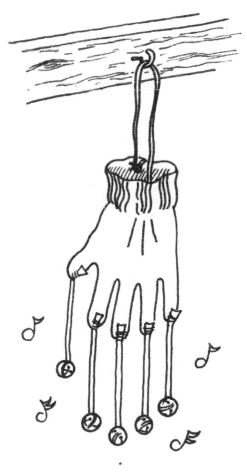

Paint Daubers

Socks/Pantyhose

Materials
pantyhose
scissors
fiberfill
yarn
paint
paper

To Make
- Cut off a 6" length of pantyhose. Cut down the length of the tube to make a rectangular piece of pantyhose.
- Place a small ball of fiberfill in the center of the rectangle.
- Pull up the edges of the pantyhose and secure them with a piece of yarn.

To Use
- Dip the paint dauber into paint, and then press it on paper to make colorful designs.

Games and
Problem
Solving

Estimation Time

Bags

Materials

plastic jars or plastic zipper-closure bags of different sizes
small objects to place into containers (such as pennies, marbles,
   paperclips, stones, seashells, erasers, or folded pieces of paper)
notebook or chart paper
marker

To Make

- Place a number of small items into clear containers, such as
  plastic jars or plastic zipper-closure bags.
- Place a notebook or piece of chart paper next to each container
  with a place for each school-ager's name and estimate.
- Clearly post the rules of the estimation game. For example: each
  child gets one guess, the closest guess without going over wins,
  opening containers is not allowed, and so on.

To Use

- School-agers estimate how many objects they think are inside
  each container. They write their guesses in the notebook or chart
  paper.
- Plan a day to open the containers and count the items inside
  each one.
- Provide prizes or certificates for winners.

Zoo Animals in Cages

 Bags

Materials
poster board
markers
scissors
permanent marker
zipper-closure plastic bags

To Make
- Draw and color a variety of animals on pieces of poster board.
- Cut out the animals.
- Use a permanent marker to draw lines on zipper-closure plastic bags to look like cages.
- Cut out wheels from poster board and put them inside the bag cages.
- Place the poster board animals inside the bags.

To Use
- The children may design a zoo or make a zoo train on a bulletin board.

Box Puzzles

 Boxes

Materials
colorful boxes (cereal, food containers)
scissors
zipper-closure plastic bags

To Make

- Cut off the front portion of each box. Then, cut the box front into interesting shapes to make a puzzle.
- Place the shapes into a zipper-closure plastic bag.

To Use

- School-agers trade puzzles with friends and challenge each other to complete the puzzles.

Mystery Boxes, Part One

 Boxes

Materials

several cardboard boxes with lids
one object for each box (Objects should reveal clues about
   themselves as they slide, roll, or make distinctive noises.)
tape
gift-wrap
chart paper
marker

To Make

- Place an object into each box.
- Tape the box securely closed.
- Wrap the box with gift-wrap.

To Use

- School-agers shake the boxes, turn them upside down, and listen to the noises to guess what is inside each box.
- Each child makes a guess about what is inside each box.
- Write all the guesses on a piece of chart paper.
- After everyone makes guesses, open the boxes to reveal the objects inside.
- Check to see how many were guessed correctly; then discuss the reasons school-agers gave for their predictions.

Mystery Boxes, Part Two

 Boxes

Materials

cardboard boxes with lids in a variety of shapes and sizes
colored craft paper
tape
scissors
black marker
yarn or string
chart paper

To Make

- Cover each box and lid with craft paper and tape it in place.
- Use a black marker to draw a large question mark on the lids of each box.
- Place a piece of string or yarn inside each box.
- Write "Mystery Box Guesses" on a sheet of chart paper.

To Use

- Each school-ager has a turn to choose a mystery box to take home. At home, he puts one thing inside the box, and then uses the string to tie the lid onto the box.
- He brings the box back the next day.
- Place the Mystery Box on a table where others can hold it, smell it, and shake it.
- After each school-ager examines the box, he guesses what is inside the box.
- Write each guess on the chart paper beside the school-ager's name.
- When everyone has had an opportunity to guess, discuss the guesses.
- The school-ager who brought the Mystery Box opens the box to reveal the contents.
- Check the chart to see if anyone made a correct guess.
- Write the correct answer at the bottom of the chart.
- Continue with another school-ager and another box.

Felt Board Box

 Boxes

Materials
felt
shoebox with lid
scissors
glue
zipper-closure plastic bags
permanent marker

To Make
- Measure and cut felt to fit the inside bottom of a shoebox.
- Glue the felt into place to make a felt board.
- Cut out a variety of story characters from felt.
- Write story titles on individual zipper-closure bags.
- Place the felt characters into the appropriately labeled bags.

To Use
- School-agers place felt characters on the shoebox felt board to tell stories.
- Store the bags of characters inside the box.

Peekscope

 Boxes

Materials
rectangular cracker box
scissors
2 identical, oblong, travel-size, unbreakable mirrors
tape

To Make
- Cut a vertical slit into one side of the box, 2" from the top.
- On the same side of the box, cut out a 2" square near the bottom of the box.

- On the opposite side of the box, cut a vertical slit 2" from the bottom of the box and a 2" square near the top.
- Insert one mirror through the top slit, so that it extends from the slit on the top of the box.
- Insert the other mirror through the bottom slit in the same fashion.
- The reflective sides of the mirrors face one another.
- Tape the mirrors securely in place.

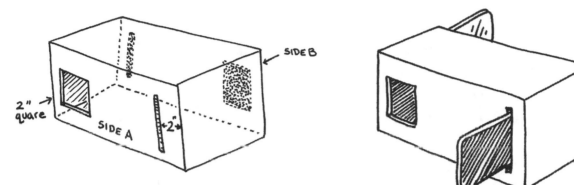

To Use

- School-agers may use the Peekscope as a "spy" tool to peek around corners.

Deck of Cards

Miscellaneous

Materials

3" x 5" unlined index cards, 2 per child
permanent markers
stencils

To Make

- Give each school-ager two index cards.
- Ask the school-agers to draw or write the same thing on both cards using permanent markers and stencils.
- Give one of the school-agers only one card to make a "wild" card.

To Use

- School-agers can use the decorated cards to create a house of cards, or they can make up card games to play with the cards.

Highest Structure Wins

Miscellaneous

Materials
building materials, such as craft sticks, straws, and clay or dough
notebook
pen or pencil
stopwatch or kitchen timer with bell

To Make
- Provide a variety of building materials for school-agers to build tall structures.
- Encourage the school-agers to set the rules of competitions for building the highest structure. Be sure to include how long a structure must stand.

To Use
- Place the materials on different tables, and determine if the school-agers will build as teams or as individuals.
- Set the timer or use the stopwatch.
- Determine winners according to time and height of structure.
- Take photographs of the winners with their structures.

Giant Checkers Sets

Miscellaneous

Materials
round cardboard inserts from frozen pizza boxes
red and black paint (or two other contrasting colors, such as orange and purple)
paintbrushes
purchased checkers set
masking tape or chalk

permanent markers, optional
large rolls of craft paper, optional

To Make

- Collect the pizza cardboards from frozen pizza boxes.
- Choose two contrasting colors of paint to use.
- Paint the cardboard pieces with a solid color on one side and a pattern of the same color on the other.
- Players should be able to flip the circle to designate that the piece has been "crowned."
- Use the purchased checkers set to determine how to draw the board on concrete outside (using chalk) or on the floor inside (using masking tape).
- School-agers may wish to create a checker board using permanent markers and large rolls of craft paper.

To Use

- School-agers can play giant checkers in teams or one on one.
- Plan large outdoor tournaments for summer fun.

Giant Chess Sets

Miscellaneous

Materials

purchased chess set
sand or gravel
12 16-ounce plastic bottles
black and white paint (or two other contrasting colors)
paintbrushes
masking tape
chalk
permanent markers, optional
large rolls of craft paper, optional

To Make

- Use the purchased chess set as a pattern for creating chess pieces and for the explanation of the rules of the game.
- Create chess pieces using various sizes and shapes of plastic bottles depending on the chess piece that is being created.
- Fill each bottle with sand or gravel to weight it down.
- Use masking tape to create details on each bottle.
- Paint the bottles and allow them to dry thoroughly.
- Create a chessboard outside on the concrete using chalk, or use masking tape on the floor inside (if space permits).
- School-agers may wish to create a chessboard using permanent markers and large rolls of craft paper.

To Use

- School-agers can play chess in teams or one on one.

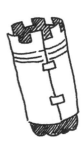  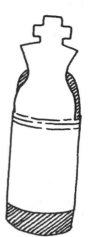 

Nature Zone

Car Litter Bag

Bags

Materials

permanent marker
gallon-size, zipper-closure plastic bag
hole punch
yarn
stickers

To Make

- Use a permanent marker to write the word "litter" on one side of the plastic bag.
- Punch a hole into each side of the bag, just below the zipper.
- Tie a piece of yarn between the holes to form a handle.
- Decorate the bag with stickers.

To Use

- School-agers hang the bag in the family car to collect litter.

Compost in a Leaf Bag

Bags

Materials

plastic leaf bag
dry leaves and grass clippings
soil
lime
water
twist-tie fastener

To Make

- Fill a leaf bag with raked leaves, grass clippings, potting soil, and a handful of lime.
- Sprinkle water over the top of the ingredients inside the bag.
- Use a twist-tie fastener to close the bag tightly.
- Flip the bag every few weeks.

To Use

- Start the compost in the autumn, and open it in time for spring planting.
- The compost is done when it is crumbly and no longer sticky.
- It should smell earthy, but not rotten.
- Use the compost for planting in pots or making a flower/vegetable garden.

Mold Garden

Bags

Materials

zipper-closure clear plastic bag

slice of white bread

water

magnifying glass

To Make

- Place the slice of bread inside the zipper-closure plastic bag.
- Dampen the bread slightly with water.
- Seal the bag, and place it in a warm place.

To Use

- School-agers watch for mold to grow on the bread.
- Use a magnifying glass to see the tiny spores.

Hanging Sponge Garden

 Bags

Materials

small sponges
water
clear plastic bag
fast-growing seeds
string
spray bottle

To Make

- Moisten the sponges with water.
- Push the seeds into the holes in the top of the sponges.
- Carefully place each sponge inside a plastic bag, with the seed side facing up.
- Tie a string loosely around the top of the bag and suspend the bag in a sunny spot.
- Open the bag and use the spray bottle to keep the sponges moist.

To Use

- Children observe the seeds sprouting.

Window Greenhouse

 Bags

Materials

paper towels
water
zipper-closure plastic bags
seeds
yarn
clothespin

To Make

- Place wet paper towels inside the plastic bag.
- Sprinkle fast-growing seeds onto the paper towel.
- Seal the bag closed.
- Stretch a length of yarn across a sunny window.
- Use a clothespin to hang the sealed bags in the window.

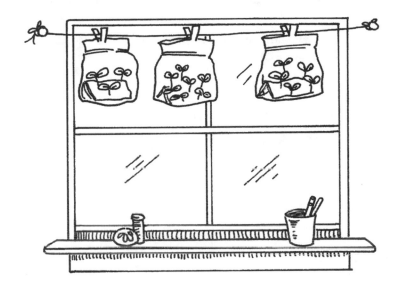

To Use

- School-agers observe the seeds sprouting and growing.

Nesting Ball

 Bags

Materials

mesh produce bag
dryer lint
yarn bits and pieces
paper scraps
fabric pieces
string or yarn

To Make

- Stuff nesting material, such as dryer lint, pieces of yarn and fabric, and paper scraps, into the mesh produce bag.
- Tie the bag closed with yarn or string.
- Hang the ball from a tree branch with a yarn loop.

To Use

- Watch for birds coming to the nesting bag for materials to build nests.
- School-agers may want to keep a journal of the birds that come to the nesting bag.

Butterfly Net

 Bags

Materials

two wire coat hangers
duct tape
masking tape
yarn
mesh produce bag

To Make

- Shape one coat hanger into a diamond shape and straighten out the handle.
- Stretch out the other hanger, so it is almost straight.
- Wrap the handles of the two hangers together and cover them with duct tape.
- Wrap a short length of masking tape around the end of a long piece of yarn to make a "needle."
- Use the yarn "needle" to lace the produce bag onto the coat hanger frame to make a net.
- Secure the bag and hangers together.

To Use

- Children use the net to capture butterflies or other insects.

Bear Caves

Bags

Materials

large paper grocery bag
scissors
stapler
fiberfill
glue
white paper
marker
small stuffed bear

To Make

- Lay the paper bag flat and cut off about 4" from the top of the bag.
- On the straight edge of the bag, cut out an arched cave opening from one side of the bag.
- Fold over the edge of the bag about 1".
- Staple along the edge to hold the fold in place.
- Pop the bag open to form a cave for a stuffed bear to use for hibernating.
- Glue some fiberfill snow along the top of the cave and along the bottom opening.
- Use white paper and a marker to make a "Do Not Disturb Until Spring" sign and glue it above the opening of the cave.
- Put a stuffed bear inside.

To Use

- Use the cave to inspire stories by school-agers.
- Provide a cassette for school-agers to record stories. Or write the stories on chart paper.

Nature Collection Display

 Bags

Materials

shoebox with lid
paint
paintbrush
construction paper
scissors
5 zipper-closure plastic bags
stapler
glue
nature items

To Make

- Paint the shoebox and lid and allow them to dry.
- Cut a piece of construction paper to fit inside each of the zipper-closure plastic bags. Line each bag with a piece of paper.
- Cut a piece of construction paper to fit inside the bottom of the box.
- Starting with the first bag, staple the piece of construction paper (that fits into the shoebox) to the side of the bag, stapling only the back of the bag behind its construction paper liner.
- Also, staple the paper along the bottom edge of the bag, through both sides of the bag.
- Staple the side of the next bag to the side of the first bag, making sure that the bag openings face in the same direction.
- Staple all of the bags together to form a strip of five bags (see illustration on the next page).
- Cut a piece of construction paper to fit inside the lid of the shoebox.
- Staple that piece to the side of the last bag in the row, stapling behind the liner.
- Staple the paper along the bottom edge through both sides of the bag.
- Glue the back paper on one end of the row of bags into the bottom of the shoebox.

- Glue the back paper on the other end of the row of bags into the lid of the shoebox.
- Let the glue dry.

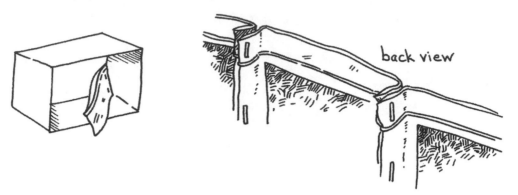

To Use

- Use tape or glue to attach natural treasures to the paper liners inside the bags.
- To store the nature collection, just fold the bags, fan-style, into the shoebox.
- To display the collection, stand the box on one end and pull out the lid away from the box to stand up the bags.

Deli Box Garden

 Boxes

Materials
clear, plastic deli box with hinged lid
potting soil
seeds
water

To Make
- Fill a clear plastic deli box with potting soil.
- Plant seeds in the soil.
- Sprinkle the soil with water.
- Close the top of the box.

To Use
- Place the box in a bright window. (Avoid direct sunlight, if possible.)
- As the sun warms the box, condensation occurs and keeps the garden watered.
- School-agers observe the garden. They may want to start a garden journal to draw changes as they happen.

Glove Garden

 Gloves/Mittens

Materials
cotton balls
water
clear, plastic food-service glove
seeds
yarn

To Make

- Place one or two wet cotton balls inside each fingertip of the glove.
- Place seeds on the cotton balls.
- Tie the opening of the glove closed with a piece of yarn.

To Use

- Hang the glove in a sunny window.
- In a few days, the seeds will start to sprout.
- School-agers might want to sketch the process each day, making a garden journal.
- School-agers may want to compare the results of this activity with the Window Greenhouse on page 100, the Hanging Sponge Garden on page 100, the Deli Box Garden on page 107, and the Sock Garden on page 108.

Sock Garden

 Socks/Pantyhose

Materials

large tube socks
aluminum baking pans
potting soil
water

To Make

- Each child pulls a tube sock over his shoe and stretches it up his leg.
- Take the children outside for a walk in a grassy field with weeds.

To Use

- After the walk, school-agers carefully remove their socks and place them into shallow pans of potting soil.
- Lightly cover the socks with soil and dampen them with water.
- Place the pans in a sunny place.
- The children watch for sprouts, keep the Sock Garden watered, and observe the kinds of plants that grow.

Bug Keeper

 Socks/Pantyhose

Materials

2-liter plastic bottle
craft knife (adults only)
pantyhose
scissors
grass clippings, twigs, and leaves
yarn

To Make

- Away from the school-agers, use a craft knife to cut off the neck of a two-liter plastic bottle. Also cut large openings into the sides of the bottle.
- Cut off one leg from a pair of pantyhose.

To Use

- School-agers place grass clippings, twigs, and leaves inside the bottle and place it inside the length of pantyhose.
- Go outside and try to capture a bug. When the school-agers capture one, they can put it inside the bottle and fasten the top of the pantyhose with a piece of yarn.
- After a day or so of observing the creature, open the top and allow it to go free.

Sprout a Pet

 Socks/Pantyhose

Materials
scissors
pantyhose
potting soil
birdseed
2 thumbtacks
hairpin
water
zipper-closure plastic bag

To Make
- Cut off one leg from a pair of pantyhose.
- Fill the foot of the stocking leg with potting soil.
- Shake the soil-filled stocking gently to help settle the soil. Then, add a little more soil to fill the foot area.
- Slide birdseed into the foot between the stocking and the dirt.
- Try to cover as much of the dirt with seeds as you can.
- Knot the stocking just above the foot to hold the dirt in place.
- Loop over the excess stocking and knot it to make a hanger for the dirt-filled foot.
- Poke two thumbtacks into the toe end of the foot for eyes.
- Slide one end of the hairpin through the top of the head and spread the two ends to look like antennae.
- Moisten the seeds with water.
- Slip the moistened critter into a plastic bag. Do not seal the bag.
- Place the bag into a dark place for a few days until the seeds start to sprout.
- When the seeds have sprouted, hang the critter in a sunny window and keep it moist.

slide birdseed between stocking and dirt.

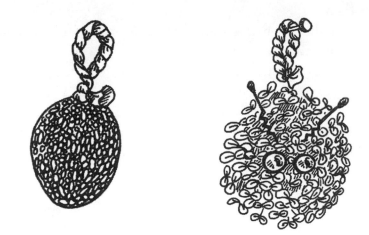

To Use

- School-agers observe the critter "growing."

Worm World

Miscellaneous

Materials

plastic aquarium
rich dark soil
water
black construction paper
tape
earthworms

To Make

- Worms make interesting classroom pets.
- Pour soil into the aquarium and add enough water so that the soil is damp, but not wet.
- Cover the sides of the aquarium with black construction paper. Tape the paper to the outside of the aquarium.
- Purchase three cartons of earthworms (wigglers work well) and dump out the cartons onto the top of the soil.
- Place a cover on the aquarium.

To Use

- Periodically observe worms by putting about one cup of soil on a table covered with craft paper.
- School-agers will enjoy having races with the worms. Be careful not to injure the worms.
- An interesting variation is to count the worms before placing them into the aquarium. Create a chart showing live and dead worms and the different dates the worms were checked.

Themes,
Special Events,
and Holidays

Salt Box Basket

 Boxes

Materials
craft knife (adults only)
salt box
paint and paintbrush
hole punch
cardboard
scissors
brad fasteners
ribbon

To Make
- Away from school-agers, use a craft knife to cut a salt box in half vertically to make two baskets.
- With the school-agers, paint one of the box halves.
- Punch a hole into each side, approximately midway around the box.
- Cut out a strip of cardboard.
- Use brad fasteners to attach the cardboard strip through the holes in the box to make a handle.
- Wind a piece of ribbon around the handle, covering it completely.
- Tie a little bow on one side of the handle.

To Use
- Fill the basket with shredded paper or artificial flowers.

Tissue Box Turkey

 Boxes

Materials

cube-shaped tissue box
toilet tissue tube
construction paper
tape
glue
scissors
craft knife (adults only)
craft sticks
dry flowers

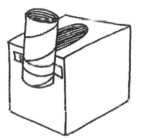

To Make

- Cover a tissue box and a toilet tissue tube with brown construction paper. Tape or glue it in place.
- Cut out the hole in the box where tissues pop out.
- Turn the box, so the opening is on top.
- Tape the tube onto one side of the box with the tube extending above the top edge of the box for the turkey's neck and head.
- Cut out eyes, a beak and a wattle from construction paper and glue the features into place.
- Cut out feathers from colored construction paper and tape each feather onto a craft stick.
- Away from school-agers, use a craft knife to cut slits into the side of the box opposite the head.
- With school-agers, place the craft stick feathers into the slits to form a colorful tail.
- Place dried or artificial flowers into the hole in the tissue box-body.

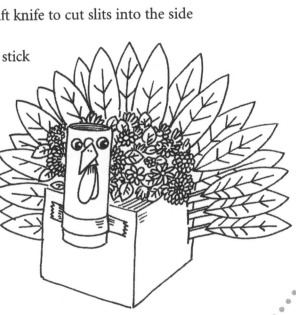

To Use

- Use the turkeys for holiday decorations or gifts.

Flower Vase

 Socks/Pantyhose

Materials

colorful sock (woman's)
scissors
empty 16 oz. can, with top removed
9 oz. plastic cup (must fit exactly inside the can)
masking tape
felt scrap
marker
glue
ribbons and trim

To Make

- Cut off the foot part of the sock.
- Cover the can using the cuff of the sock, covering the rim of the can with the elastic end of the cuff.
- Push the plastic cup down into the can to hold the sock in place at the top.
- Use masking tape to tape the bottom of the sock flat against the bottom of the can.
- Trace around the bottom of the can onto the felt scrap.
- Cut out the circle and glue it onto the bottom of the can.
- Glue ribbon and trim onto the can to decorate it.

To Use

- Place real or artificial flowers into the vase.

Stuffed Apple

 Socks/Pantyhose

Materials
white sock
scissors
fiberfill
rubber band
red and green paint
paintbrushes
green felt scrap
hole punch
green yarn

To Make
- Cut a 5" piece from the toe end of the sock.
- Stuff the toe section with fiberfill to make a round apple shape.
- Close the opening the sock with a rubber band.
- Paint the round part of the apple red.
- Paint the excess sock above the rubber band green and twist it into a stem while it is still wet.
- Allow the apple and stem to dry completely.
- Cut out a leaf shape from green felt.
- Punch a hole into the base of the leaf.
- Cut off an 8" piece of green yarn.
- Thread the leaf onto the yarn and tie it to the base of the apple stem.
- Wrap the yarn around the rubber band to conceal it.
- Tie the ends together to hold the leaf and yarn in place.

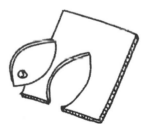

cut a leaf shape from green felt....

To Use
- Display the apples in a basket or bowl.
- Also, add apples to the drama zone for added interest.

Soft Sculpture Pumpkin

 Socks/Pantyhose

Materials

2 pairs of pantyhose
scissors
stapler
fiberfill
2 rubber bands
orange and green paint
paintbrushes
brown or green pipe cleaners
pencil
green tissue paper
glue

To Make

- Cut off the four legs of the two pairs of pantyhose.
- Cut off the toe ends of the hose, so that all four legs are open at the ends.
- Arrange the legs crossing over each other at the center, like the spokes of a wheel.
- Staple the legs together at the point where they all cross over each other.
- Stuff all eight sections of pantyhose with fiberfill.
- Stuff toward the center, leaving the last 6" from each leg opening without stuffing.
- Pull up the eight sections and around to the center to form a pumpkin shape.
- Hold the sections together with a rubber band.
- Braid or twist the excess stocking ends together to make a stem for the pumpkin.
- Hold the ends in place with a second rubber band.
- Fluff and pull the sections together to make the sections fit together without gaps.
- Paint the pumpkin orange and the stem green. Allow it to dry.

- Wrap pipe cleaners around a pencil to make spirals.
- Remove the pencil and push the spirals into the pumpkin near the stem and glue into place.
- Cut out green tissue paper leaves and glue them around the stem.

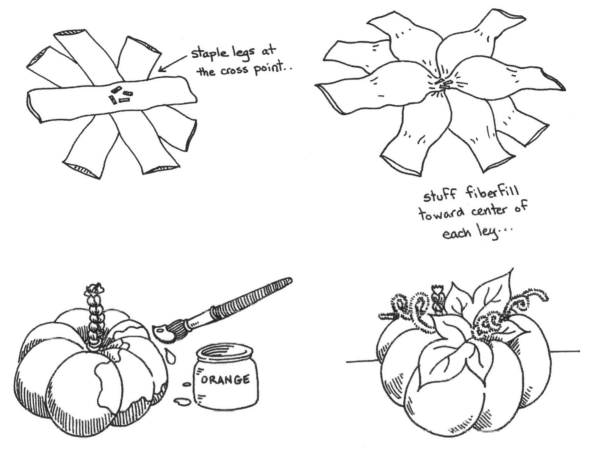

staple legs at the cross point..

stuff fiberfill toward center of each leg...

ORANGE

To Use

- Display as pumpkins or use black felt to make jack-o-lantern faces on them.

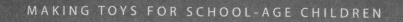

Teacher Tips

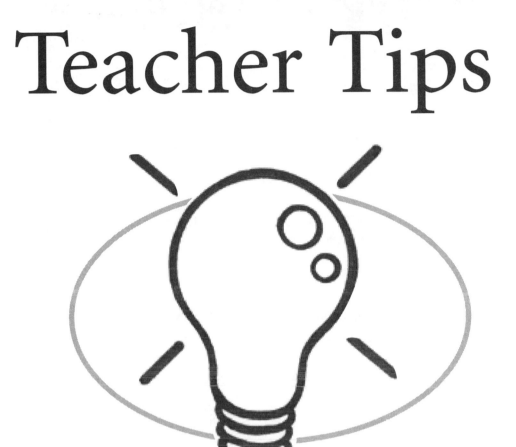

Paper Scrap Bag

 Bags

Materials
paper grocery bag
tape

To Make
- Tape a paper grocery bag to the edge of a table where school-agers are cutting paper.

To Use
- For easy cleanup after a cutting project, school-agers push paper scraps from the table into the bag.
- Label the bag and save the paper scraps for another art project.

Water Toy Organizer

Bags

Materials
water toys
mesh produce bag
twine or ribbon

To Make
- Place wet water toys inside a mesh produce bag.
- If the bag has no closure, string twine or ribbon in and out of the top of the mesh bag.

To Use
- Hang the bag of wet toys over the water table, sink, or outside to drip and air-dry.
- The mesh bag allows the toys to be visible for choosing, while keeping them organized.

Yarn Bags

 Bags

Materials
construction paper
scissors
mesh produce bags
pipe cleaner

To Make
- Roll yarn into balls.
- Place the balls of yarn inside a mesh produce bag.
- Thread the ends of yarn through the holes to dangle from the bottom of the bag.
- Twist a pipe cleaner around the opening of the bag.

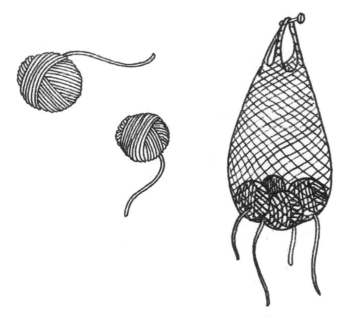

To Use
- Hang the bag at a convenient level.
- Pull on a strand of yarn and cut it.
- Storing yarn this way keeps it untangled, and yarn balls are visible for choosing desired colors.

Plastic Grocery Bag Smocks

 Bags

Materials

plastic grocery bags with attached handles
scissors

To Make

- Cut off the bottom of the plastic bag.
- Cut open the bag from the bottom to the opening, making a vest.

To Use

- School-agers slip their arms through the handles to use the bags as disposable smocks.

Birdseed Bag Pictures

 Bags

Materials

large, empty birdseed bag
scissors
large boxes, optional
glue, optional

To Make

- Cut out pictures from the outside layer of the birdseed bags because the inside part may have oily spots from the sunflower and thistle seeds.

To Use

- Glue the pictures onto large boxes for child-sized birdhouses, or use them to decorate the classroom for a bird-related theme.

Paper Bag Labels

 Bags

Materials

markers or paint and paintbrushes
large paper grocery bags
newspapers
tape

To Make

- Use markers or paint to write the words for the label in the center of one wide side of a bag.
- Use only lower-case block print (for example, nature collection).
- Stuff the bag with crumpled newspapers.
- Fold the opening closed and tape the fold securely closed.

To Use

- Use these three-dimensional labels anywhere that labels are normally found, including display tables, science centers, or book areas.

Work Displays

 Bags

Materials

school-ager's artwork or writing
1- and 2-gallon zipper-closure plastic bags
hole punch
yarn
scissors

To Make

- Place the artwork or writing inside individual bags and seal the bags.
- Punch holes into the four corners of each bag.
- Tie the bags together with yarn, so that one bag hangs from another.

To Use

- Hang these displays on doors, in the hallway, from the ceiling, or side by side across the room as a way to display school-agers' work.

Bulletin Board Displays

 Boxes

Materials
small cardboard boxes
colored contact paper, optional
stapler

To Make
- If desired, cover the small cardboard boxes with colored contact paper.
- Staple the bottoms of small cardboard boxes onto a bulletin board.

To Use
- Display three-dimensional artwork inside the boxes.
- If the names and the dates are on the backs of the art creations, make labels with the school-ager's name and date and place them underneath each box.

Disposable Paint Cups

 Boxes

Materials
small milk cartons, waxed
scissors
paint

To Make
- Use scissors to cut off the tops of the milk cartons.

To Use
- Fill the milk cartons with paint.
- When the school-agers finish painting, they can empty the leftover paint into storage jars and toss away the empty cartons.
- No messy cleanup!

Paintbrush Holder

 Boxes

Materials
cardboard toilet tissue rolls
shoebox
tape
paintbrushes

To Make
- Collect enough cardboard toilet tissue rolls to fill a shoebox.
- Stand the rolls upright inside an open shoebox.
- Tape the rolls together, and then tape them to the shoebox.

To Use
- Sort and store paintbrushes, brush side up, in the tubes.

Song Box

 Boxes

Materials
poster board
scissors
markers
clear contact paper
small cardboard box
art supplies

To Make
- Cut out strips from poster board.
- Write favorite song titles on the poster board strips with a marker.
- Cover the strips with clear contact paper.
- Decorate the cardboard box using markers or other art supplies.

To Use
- Place the song title strips inside the box.
- Select a strip from the box.
- This is a fair way to choose songs to sing.
- The same system can work well for games.

Bulletin Board Pockets

 Boxes

Materials
colored contact paper
scissors
fast-food French fry boxes
stapler

To Make

- Cut colored contact paper to fit around French fry boxes.
- Cover the fry holders with the contact paper.

To Use

- Staple the fry holders onto a bulletin board for pockets to hold game pieces, nature collections, flannel board pieces, or small puppets.

Construction Paper Storage

 Boxes

Materials

several same-size cardboard cereal boxes
craft knife (adults only)
tape
different colors of construction paper

To Make

- Away from school-agers, use a craft knife to remove the tops from the cereal boxes.
- With the school-agers, stack the boxes one on top of the other, with the wide sides together.
- Tape the boxes securely together.

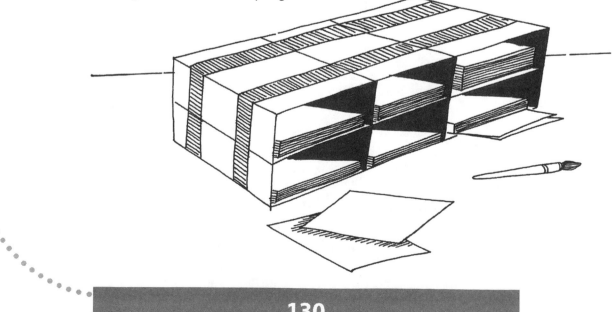

To Use

- Sort colored construction paper into individual boxes for each color.
- Place the paper organizer in easy reach of the art table.

Copy Paper Box Storage

 Boxes

Materials

copy paper boxes
colored contact paper
notebook paper
tape
permanent markers

To Make

- Copy paper boxes make excellent storage units.
- Cover the boxes with colored contact paper, which will make them last longer.
- Tape a piece of notebook paper to the end of the box to make a label for it.
- Also, make a list of the materials stored in the box and tape it to the inside of the box.

To Use

- Store the boxes of materials on shelves or on the floor. The boxes will stack nicely.
- Arrange the boxes so that you can see the labels.

Nature Collection Containers

 Boxes

Materials
colored construction paper
scissors
cardboard, Styrofoam, or plastic hamburger or salad containers
tape
colored permanent markers
nature items

To Make
- Cut construction paper to fit around the hamburger or salad boxes.
- Tape the construction paper around the boxes. Use markers to decorate them.
- Place nature items inside the covered hamburger boxes.
- Use a marker to label each box's contents.

To Use
- Use the labeled boxes to display a nature collection or to store hard-to-find nature items.

Card Game Organizers

 Boxes

Materials
markers
white adhesive labels
scissors
picture label of card game, optional
glue
plastic or metal bandage boxes
cards

To Make

- Draw a picture of the card game on a white adhesive label, or cut out a picture of the card game from the original card game label.
- Attach the picture label to the front of the plastic or metal adhesive bandage box.
- On the back of the box, attach a white label with the rules of the game or just the number of cards that should be in the box.

To Use

- Place game cards inside the labeled bandage box.
- Plastic or metal boxes are more durable than the cardboard boxes that the cards come in.

Box Lid Games

 Boxes

Materials

construction paper
scissors
box lids (large boot box lids, office supply box lids, storage box lids)
glue
stickers, markers, and art supplies
dice, spinners, or playing cards
buttons

To Make

- Cut construction paper to fit inside the lid of a box.
- Cover the inside of the box lid with the construction paper and glue it in place.
- Use stickers, markers, and other art supplies to create winding paths, a starting point, and an end.
- Add dice, spinners, or movement cards to move button tokens along the paths.

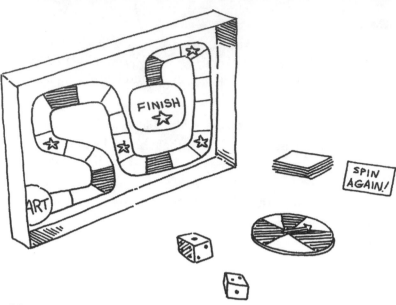

To Use

- School-agers play the simple games with a friend or two.
- Games may be theme-related, reflect children's interests, or encourage skill development.

No-Mess Paint Trays

Miscellaneous

Materials
clean, empty yogurt cups with snap-on lids
thick, cardboard beverage trays from fast-food restaurants
craft knife (adults only)
paint
paintbrushes

To Make
- Place yogurt cups into the beverage holder cups.
- Away from the school-agers, use a craft knife to cut out a hole in the lids just large enough for a paintbrush to fit through.

To Use
- Fill the yogurt cups with paint.
- Snap on the lids and place paintbrushes inside the holes.
- No-Mess Paint Trays make fewer spills, less wasted paint, and no mess!

Dear Parents,

We need your help to create wonderful toys. Please send any of the materials that are checked. All materials should be thoroughly clean and dry.

Thank you!

- ☐ Adhesive labels, white
- ☐ Aluminum foil
- ☐ Birdseed
- ☐ Book rings
- ☐ Bottle caps and lids
- ☐ Box lids
- ☐ Brad fasteners
- ☐ Bubble wrap
- ☐ Buttons
- ☐ Cardboard boxes
- ☐ Cardboard tubes
- ☐ Cellophane
- ☐ Cereal boxes
- ☐ Chalk
- ☐ Checkers set
- ☐ Clay
- ☐ Clothespins, wooden
- ☐ Confetti
- ☐ Construction paper
- ☐ Contact paper, clear or patterned
- ☐ Copy paper boxes
- ☐ Cotton balls
- ☐ Cotton gloves
- ☐ Craft feathers
- ☐ Craft sticks
- ☐ Crayons
- ☐ Crepe paper streamers
- ☐ Dice
- ☐ Duct tape
- ☐ Erasers
- ☐ Fabric
- ☐ Fabric paint

- ☐ Felt
- ☐ Food coloring
- ☐ Gardening gloves
- ☐ Gift boxes
- ☐ Gloves, all sizes
- ☐ Glue
- ☐ Golf tees
- ☐ Hole punch
- ☐ Ice cream cartons
- ☐ Index cards
- ☐ Jingle bells
- ☐ Kitchen timer
- ☐ Lace
- ☐ Magazines
- ☐ Magnetic strips
- ☐ Magnifying glasses
- ☐ Markers
- ☐ Masking tape
- ☐ Mesh produce bags
- ☐ Milk cartons, assorted sizes
- ☐ Mirror, unbreakable
- ☐ Mittens, all sizes
- ☐ Neckties
- ☐ Newspaper
- ☐ Oatmeal container
- ☐ Paint
- ☐ Paintbrushes
- ☐ Pantyhose
- ☐ Paper cups
- ☐ Paper grocery bags
- ☐ Paper lunch bags
- ☐ Paper plates
- ☐ Permanent markers
- ☐ Pie tins

- ☐ Pipe cleaners
- ☐ Plaster of Paris
- ☐ Plastic bags, all sizes
- ☐ Plastic bottles and jars
- ☐ Pompoms
- ☐ Popsicle sticks
- ☐ Ribbon
- ☐ Rubber bands
- ☐ Salt boxes
- ☐ Seashells
- ☐ Sequins
- ☐ Shoeboxes, with and without lids
- ☐ Shoestrings
- ☐ Socks, all sizes
- ☐ Sponges
- ☐ Spray paint
- ☐ Staplers
- ☐ Stickers
- ☐ Straws, drinking
- ☐ Styrofoam balls, 2 ½"
- ☐ Tempera paint
- ☐ Tissue boxes
- ☐ Tissue paper
- ☐ Tube socks, all sizes
- ☐ Tweezers
- ☐ Twine
- ☐ Velcro
- ☐ Watercolors
- ☐ Wiggle eyes
- ☐ Wire clothes hangers
- ☐ Wrapping paper
- ☐ Yarn

Index